GROUP
EDUCATION
FOR A
DEMOCRACY

Published under the Auspices of the

AMERICAN ASSOCIATION FOR THE STUDY OF GROUP WORK

PUBLICATIONS COMMITTEE:

James E. Brockway   Louis Kraft
Neva R. Deardorff   Agnes B. Leahy, *Secretary*
Abel J. Gregg   Joshua Lieberman, *Chairman*
Charles E. Hendry   S. R. Slavson
Clara A. Kaiser   Arthur L. Swift, Jr.

GROUP EDUCATION
FOR A
DEMOCRACY

by
WILLIAM HEARD KILPATRICK

ASSOCIATION PRESS
347 Madison Avenue   New York
1940

PRINTED IN THE UNITED STATES OF AMERICA

INTRODUCTION

THIS book is a collection of articles that have for the most part appeared in various educational journals. Most have been more or less revised for inclusion here, some to bring them up to date, others to make them fit together in serving the present purposes of publication. (The original source of publication is given in each instance. Where none is mentioned, the article is appearing in print for the first time.) As originally written, most of the chapters here appearing were addressed to teachers or others engaged in school work; some, however, were delivered before organizations engaged in young people's club work.

The book is designed to meet the needs of any who are interested in the education of "teen-age" young people, whether in the home or in school or in club work. The emphasis accordingly is on the education that goes on among adolescents as they associate together. One purpose, then, of the book is to bring parents, teachers, and group workers closer together as they respectively work with their young people. All three sets of elders work simultaneously with the same youth. Their aims should accordingly concur, and their efforts should follow the same psychological principles. That they may not work at cross purposes, it is essential that they so understand each other as to bring about effective co-operation.

The social and psychological orientations of the book will early manifest themselves to the discerning reader.

189918

Socially, the fundamental position taken is that of democracy, of democracy understood as the effort to run society on a basis of ethics. This democratic interest looks in two directions: one toward equality of opportunity in life, including in particular equal opportunity in the economic field; the other toward the development of individuals more adequately capable and disposed to manage life, particularly in social matters.

As matters now stand, the economic problem is crucial to individual and social welfare. This does not mean that life is primarily economic, any more than that man is primarily physical; but that an unhealthy economy insistently upsets social life much as an unhealthy body insistently upsets individual life. As long as either evil state lasts, it makes insistent demands for attention; where either has been restored to proper health, attention can then be given to other and higher concerns. Any who have to do with youth must understand how economic conditions peculiarly concern adolescents, granting or withholding as they do morale-building opportunities for normal life work and marriage. Youth are, besides, further concerned here, because it is they who must in a half-generation begin to take effective charge of social and political affairs. It is these considerations that explain the social emphasis appearing in the book.

The fundamental psychological orientation of the book is toward the development of social and moral characters through and by the exercise, under wise guidance, of responsible living in association. This outlook stands in essential contrast with a psychology of learning which, based on conditioning and drill, puts decisions primarily if not exclusively in the hands of parents, teachers, and leaders and looks to docile acceptance on the part of youth to fix the wisdom of age in their otherwise empty and incompetent minds and characters.

The position herein taken is that learning necessarily goes on in all active experiencing—being essential in fact to make experience out of otherwise mere happenings. So that, therefore, further and better insight and conduct on the part of the young must grow out of the exercise of their best available present insight and conduct. In this way the psychological outlook is itself as truly democratic as was the social. This does not mean that it is psychologically impossible to train and indoctrinate youth on a basis of externally authoritative conditioning and drill—existing dictatorship education is proof to the contrary. But it does mean that such indoctrination and training cannot give the requisite preparation for living in a democracy. Besides, fortunately for democracy, the more socially responsible types of self-directed activity are in the long run more educationally effective.

A word may be said about group work, since this book is being published under the auspices of the American Association for the Study of Group Work. The author takes responsibility here for stating his personal opinion, assisted at points by publications of the Association, that group work is a highly worthy new interest, whether this go on in school classes or in recreation and other informal education. This group work is, however, not to be thought of as a separate field of work, but rather as a method to be used in all kinds of educational effort. "Group work" in this sense is just now more or less of a movement, and as such deserves support and success. But its success will be achieved when, and to the degree that, effective working in groups has established itself as an essential part of any adequate education of youth, however and wherever conducted. The older school was unduly and unwisely individualistic, and accordingly failed to be adequately educative. The new group work will properly help to correct this older individualistic emphasis.

In conclusion, certain words of personal appreciation are appropriate. That this book has come into existence at all is due to the suggestion and active efforts of Mr. Joshua Lieberman, of the Association interested in group work. That it is as good as it is is due to the sympathetic insight of Dr. Marion Y. Ostrander, who contributed largely to Parts II and III by helping to choose what should appear, revising many of the articles (or seeing that the author revised them), editing all so as to make a consistent whole, and finally by seeing the book through the press. To Mr. S. M. Keeny, of the Association Press, best thanks are due for his responsible supervision of the whole enterprise.

W. H. K.

May 1, 1940.

CONTENTS

Part I

THE DEMANDS OF THE SOCIAL SITUATION TODAY

I

WHAT IS DEMOCRACY?*

DEMOCRACY is at once a faith, a hope, and a program. As originally conceived, democracy was a matter of government, a faith that men in the aggregate could be trusted to govern themselves; and only a short time ago this faith seemed about to conquer the world. Now matters are different. Many there are in various countries who assert that men cannot be so trusted. These have given up faith in democracy.

But still there are many, very many in many countries, who yet stand ready to stake their future on making democracy true. These go on further to say that government is not enough. Democracy must mean, besides, that both man and men, humanity and the many human individuals, have potentialities that constitute the most fundamental objective of human endeavor—each of all men to count as one. The plain facts, however, compel us to admit that no man has yet seen the realization of

* *Childhood Education,* March, 1938.

human potentialities—of some, yes; of all, no. These realizations of necessity belong to the future, possibly to an ever-receding future. The will, however, at once to believe in such potentialities and to stake our lives on realizing them—this is, in truth, a faith—a daring and a noble faith. We who accept it pledge therein all we hold sacred to make this faith come true.

Fortunately, this democracy is not an unsupported faith. It is a hope; in fact, a grounded hope. Where democracy has seemingly failed, there it has had no adequate trial. On the other hand, its greatest successes have been where it has been tried longest. To build a culture adequate to maintain democracy requires a long time and favoring conditions. These neither Germany nor Italy nor Russia had known. No autocracy, however, whether of one man or a few, has ever succeeded in finding a method to transmit itself in strength. Unlimited power to rule over others becomes at length selfish and reckless. It then fails. So past history has it. So the future promises.

Present dictatorships depend on holding the people in subjection to dictated ideas and beliefs, excluding all contrary ideas from abroad. But intercommunication is impossible to prevent altogether. For one thing, the knowledge and science necessary to run the modern world will find a way for repressed humanity to know across the borders what others know, and so at length to think what others think. We who believe in democracy have real grounds for hoping and believing that in the long run only democracy can survive.

But democracy can hope to survive only as it bases itself on an adequate program. It must be true to itself. We profess to believe in the sacredness of human personality; we must then devise procedures and institutions that do in fact respect and realize this personality. The whole culture must consistently so act. At the present time industry exactly denies this. Men trade on the theory of downing one another, and factories are run primarily to produce goods even at the expense of personality. Democracy must remake such an industry or itself decay.

As for the schools, we in them must find ways of enthroning democracy in all their works. As it is, schoolroom and school system are but too often benevolent autocracies. A line-and-staff administration, borrowed from the army, seeks to turn out a mass production of learning, essentially on a factory basis. We cannot in such ways expect to teach democracy. Only as it is lived can it be learned. Specifically, every school procedure must embody democracy, and all concerned with any decision should share, actually, in the making of it. On this basis alone should teachers work and pupils study.

From these various considerations we conclude that democracy is a faith not yet thoroughly accepted, a hope as yet only partially justified, and a program that largely remains to be made. What is thus lacking exactly defines our duty.

II

EDUCATION AND THE
SOCIAL SITUATION

I. *The deeper problems of any school system in respect of aim, method, and curriculum are set for us by the social situation of which the system is part; and the answers to these problems must be sought in terms of the facts and possibilities of this actual developing situation.*

Any modern nation or group builds its school system partly out of love for its children, partly out of concern for the group welfare. Either attitude must, if intelligently pursued, lead to a study of the surrounding social situation. The children will live in that situation; they must accordingly learn to deal with it. The group welfare is bound up in the possibilities of the situation, and must likewise be sought in terms of those possibilities. On no other basis than a study of this situation could pertinent aims be set up for the educational system, or suitable means (e.g., method and curriculum) be chosen for it. Out of such study will arise the more fundamental problems of any school system. All other educational problems, whether of support or control, are logically subordinate to these.

But no actual situation, particularly in modern times, remains fixed or static. It develops under our eyes as we study it. Proper analysis will show certain factors at work in the situation as more significant than others;

4

also, some of these promise to remain important for a longer time than others. On these more abiding and significant factors any intelligent planning will found itself. It is such facts and the possibilities growing out of them that must determine the character of any educational system that we would build.

II. *Although the achievements of our American civilization and culture are in comparison with others highly significant, it still remains true that our present social situation is seriously awry.*

When millions are out of work and many millions beyond these feel helpless and insecure as they face the future, something is seriously wrong. We have vastly more machinery and power at our disposal than ever before, but even so there is unprecedented failure and uncertainty. And our evils are not simply financial and economic. There is wide-spread crime. Graft and dishonesty are all too common in our politics. Ugliness vaunts itself throughout the country. And as for morals and religion, never before were so large a proportion of any people so uncertain as to what to think and believe on fundamental matters. Truly, our situation is seriously awry.

III. *The crucial element and factor that most accounts for this existing evil state of affairs is, it seems safe to assert, our unsatisfactory economic system.*

Thus, to see our economic and business system as the present strategic evil is neither to profess nor admit a creed of materialism.

Nor is it to say that the economic is under normal conditions the most important element in life. It is like a man with a serious digestive upset. For him to give principal attention to recovery is no sign that his god is his belly. What he is trying to do is to reduce the upsetting disturbance to proper functioning and oblivion in order that he may rightfully give first place to finer and more important things. So now with the economic factor. It has got out of order. It thus upsets nearly everything else. When we shall have straightened it out and so have reduced it to its proper subordination, then civilization too can give first place to finer and better things.

That our evil economic system is the crucial element and factor in our other ills is not difficult to believe. When, as was true a century and a half ago, 90 per cent of our people lived on farms and each family raised and made by far the most of what it consumed, when further there was limitless land awaiting new settlers on the cheapest terms—under such conditions each man could, if he would but work, hope to become economically independent. The American Dream was in large measure realized. But when power machinery was introduced and division of labor came to prevail, especially as corporations grew ever larger and an ever larger proportion of our population accepted the permanent status of employees, when even farmers have come to buy the most of what they consumed—since all this has become true, the old independence has ceased. Dependence, or perhaps better interdependence, has become the rule. For now almost every one must sell either goods or services to get the money wherewith to buy what he has need of, and he can sell neither goods nor services unless market conditions warrant. So all of us have become together dependent on "market conditions," on the well-working of the economic system as one whole. When, as in the depression, the economic business system breaks down, all suffer together. The poor lose their positions, while the rich lose their dividends and often their whole fortunes. Interdependence has become only too cruelly true.

Now a common interdependence calls for a common co-operative effort to take care of the common welfare; but business is still trying to run itself on the old basis of competitive struggle for profits. It knows no other way. A fundamental split thus holds in the very vitals of our social life: in terms of the new conditions, co-operation for the common welfare is demanded; in terms of business and its outmoded methods, each man is called upon to seek his own welfare without regard to the welfare of others—if need be even at the expense of their welfare.

Ethics in such a divided culture falls into war with itself. From the broader point of view—and every higher religion sees this—each one should work for the good of all together, loving his neighbor as himself. But from the point of view of existing business conditions of livelihood and the care of one's family and dependents, each one must seek through available business processes to earn a living and prepare against the time of sickness and old age. Now no one can work consistently along both these lines. The two are irreconcilable. Society is ethically at war with itself.

Moreover, it becomes very easy for our youth, who

grow up amid our wide-spread applause for success at money getting, to become careless of the means used for heaping up riches.   If parents are already careless in such—and unfortunately many are—the children readily think that "everybody does it."   Dishonesty easily grows, and especially where speculation is common.   For speculation is very, very close to gambling and stealing.   All three involve trying to get money without rendering service.

And still further, when government has economic favors to grant to its favorites, the temptation is very strong to build political machines to control and dispense the favors—for a consideration.   Thus business gets into politics.   Graft in local politics follows tariff favors in national politics—and politics easily becomes corrupt.

It is not necessary to continue the argument.   Turn where we will, the story is the same.   The competitive struggle for profits at the expense of others—this brings on depressions and otherwise prevents our industrial system from working to capacity.   The same competitive struggle for profits degrades our ethical outlook—hardly even the highest can escape at least some hurt here.   The same struggle also educates multitudes of the young and the weak to dishonesty.   Still further, since beauty costs more, we are beset on all sides with public ugliness.   All through life the competitive struggle, which turns man against man, degrades and must degrade.   It is this that constitutes the crucial and principal factor to account for the present evil state of our social situation.

IV. *Although social change is always in process, especially under modern conditions, still we seem warranted in believing that mankind stands now at the threshold of unusual reconstruction, at the very beginning of a new cultural epoch.*

The term "reconstruction" as here used is meant to refer to such an epochal change in social and institutional forms and outlook as introduces essentially a new era—such that historians in the distant future will call attention to this period as the time when an outstanding era began. The reasons for thinking this are not difficult to accept. Chiefly and most fundamentally, they relate to epochal changes in scientific knowledge and processes, and consequently to probably unprecedented industrial changes that must bring profound social changes. Until the steam engine (1767), muscular power of man or beast did most of the world's work. With steam harnessed to the new machines, modern industry came into existence; but even so most of the available energy in the coal was wasted. Since 1900, however, great advances have been made in the utilization and transmission of energy, so that man has freed for actual use, so it is estimated, more energy in this one generation than in all the years in human history before. And we have only begun. Other applications of science promise like revolutions in many, many industrial processes already, including at many points agriculture itself.

These things mean, for one thing, that for the first time in history man can make enough goods for everybody. Always hitherto there has not been enough to go around. Some had to go hungry if any lived well.

Now henceforth, if we but act intelligently, all can have both security and plenty. All can cultivate and enjoy the good life. When we couple the foregoing possibilities with the facts of more wide-spread education than ever existed before and the unprecedented means of communication and popularization now available, together with the further fact of more wide-spread unrest and agitation to bring a better state of affairs into being than the world has ever known before—when we consider all these, it seems reasonable to believe that some nation will lead off and the others will watch and follow. Selfish interests may resist for awhile; but if a way out can be seen, sooner or later men will accept and apply it. The new era will begin.

V. *This incoming social state must found itself economically and socially on the outstanding new degree of interdependence; it must expect to proceed by means of a high degree of inclusive social planning.*

The fact of economic interdependence was shown in the paragraphs above to be so significant that it cannot be disregarded. If any nation tries to ignore it, the economic processes of that nation will falter and fail. For a few years it may be possible to ignore this factor of interdependence, and our country may unwisely make the effort; but when so much turns on this interdependence—depressions, for example—men will learn to regard it. The selfish few may be willing to disregard it in order to maintain their existing privileges, but the welfare of the many will eventually prevail. Intelligence will call attention to the fact, and the public will eventually learn.

Analogously for planning. The fact of interdependence calls for a planning commensurate with the degree
of interdependence. We have always had planning—of
individual men, of voluntary corporations, and of nations. It is no more than the application of intelligence
to the enterprise at hand on terms that intelligence can
grasp. And this is our hope. The intelligent co-ordina-
tion of otherwise warring effort can manifestly accomplish
more than without it would obtain. We may then expect
an intelligent people eventually to see the greater possibilities and demand their realization. As said above in
other connections, selfish efforts will doubtless be made
to stem the tide. But eventually the intelligent way will
in America win out, especially if other nations meanwhile
are showing the way.

VI. *Amid all the changes that impend, there appears
no sufficient reason why America should give up its essential democracy, and, in the judgment and hope of this
writer, every reason to the contrary. We must cherish
our democratic regard for personality as such and continue to hold fast to the democratic doctrine of government by the consent of the governed.*

Many things can be said in connection. We have
never had any thoroughgoing democracy, but that is no
reason why we should not now come closer to it. Our
precise form of government may not be the best; it
probably must be improved. But, if changes be needed,
amending the Constitution or holding a new constitutional convention would be exactly and precisely the
democratic procedure called for. Any less or different
would be undemocratic. The idea that that Constitu-

tion is too sacred to be changed is a most undemocratic doctrine.   To act on it would be to make tyrants of the founding fathers.

In thus advocating democracy, we do so not simply or primarily because democracy has come down to us through the American tradition.   Any tradition always needs sifting, and some elements of it must from time to time be rejected.   The claims for democracy are better founded: namely, on the criticized results of human association through thousands of years.   The highest available ethical theory demands respect for personality.   The free play of intelligence in human affairs demands freedom of thought and speech, in order that the best may be found and spread.   History seems to show that the popular government is the surest guarantee of both.

III

WATCHMAN, WHAT OF THE NIGHT?*

THE inquiry at this time is not of the international situation, dark though that be. Nor is it directly of the business outlook, though that remains sullenly stagnant. The inquiry here is of the general social-economic-political situation in this country and its present movement. Considering where we wish developments to lead us, the question is as to whether we seem to be moving satisfactorily in the desired direction; and if not, what factors are at work to thwart our aims, and what, accordingly, should we do?

First of all, where do we wish developments to carry us? It may clarify further thinking if we restate our aims, even though we do no more than repeat what has already been many times said.

The answer here to be given as to aims is precisely a restatement of the conception and aims of democracy itself. We wish our civilization to move more definitely toward a regime of effectual respect for personality and this on honest terms of equality so far as it is humanly possible to effect it. As our ancestors rejected any and all programs for hereditary privilege and external control, so do we now. We not only agree with them in rejecting external political control of the many by the

_____

* *Social Frontier,* February, 1939.

few; we also wish to abolish the economic control of the many by the few. We agree with them in rejecting hereditary privileges of government and feudal class; we wish again to go further and abolish hereditary privileges of wealth, with their entailed special access to economic security and cultural advantages. It is an honest effort at equality of opportunity that we seek. In any changes that may be brought about, we wish not so much a leveling down as a leveling up, for we believe that we now have available resources of procedures and raw materials sufficient to bring, in time, comfort and security to all. Finally, in any efforts at making changes we wish to rely on the democratic-educative processes of free and fair discussion registering itself in a free ballot. *We have no faith in the effort to bring about democratic ends by undemocratic measures of violence and indoctrination.*

Advances Are Real, Albeit Slow

With these democratic aims and procedures before us, what of the situation? Are we moving satisfactorily in the direction thus indicated? If we had some way of taking a poll of the country on the general situation, including aims as well as movements, it would be a confused reply that we should probably get. As to the aims set out above, some among us would answer no, others yes, and possibly the larger number would hesitate. If we could have taken a poll in 1926, say, so that we could now compare its answers with those of 1939, we should probably find a trend: the proportion voting yes in 1939 on the aims as stated above would be larger. The country has moved. Depression and discussion and governmental experimentation have together moved a considerable proportion of the people in the direction of the aims stated.

Granted some movement, has it been satisfactory? Although the answer depends partly on what one had expected, it is still probably true that many who most wish such a movement would be the first to say no; the movement so far is not satisfactory. A very great distance remains to be covered before conditions are tolerable on any terms of honest equality. For far too many among us life denies even the essentials, except on degrading terms of governmental aid. For the majority of us all, conditions still deny security and comfort, even though these be theoretically possible. Even if the movement be in the desirable direction, it is still very, very slow.

Why is the movement so slow? Is it because the few who enjoy social privileges manage by a control of press, radio, moving pictures, churches, and the like to prevent the many from understanding their own good? There is something to this, but more likely the hindrance lies chiefly deeper: that is, in the culture, in the surrounding culture which so pervasively molds us to its model. When a whole people, as did ours in great part for some three hundred years, act on the firm belief that each should make it his rule to seek his own individualistic good and let the common good take care of itself, and when on this belief as a foundation, these people build their dominant institutions and construct their theory of rights—when these things are so, we cannot expect any one decade to introduce great changes. From this point of view, the movement has not been so slow. It is perhaps remarkable that so much has been accomplished.

A Positive Program of Action

What then of the future? In particular, what should we do? The answer seems to lie in making a program compounded of immediate and long-time efforts. Immediately, the aim is to consolidate and advance the social gains made in recent years, protecting them against attack from both parties. This includes healing the breach within labor and otherwise maintaining the morale of those seeking a real new deal.

The long-term program is even more important. So long as our culture is no stronger in the critical consideration of what one accepts, just so long we cannot hope to gain as much as we should like from discussions with those now in middle life. They have, too many of them, not only fixed what they believe, but in too many instances have barred the doors against listening to the other side. Our hope must mainly lie with younger men and women and with the rising generation. For this, two things seem necessary. On the one hand, we must have the best possible critical thinking at the intellectual top so as to furnish the best possible stuff for discussion purposes lower down in the age and intelligence scale. On the other hand, we must have in school, college, and adult forums full and free study and discussion. Let it be emphasized that it is study and not indoctrination that is here sought. We need study all up and down the line, partly because we do not yet know how to solve our social-economic-political problem, partly because it is only by personal study that one can build the personal intelligence needed to share effectively in changing the social situation. Most people have sufficient native ability to become intelligent if only they will but keep at it.

How long will it take to make substantial changes? Nobody knows. War may come and upset all calculations, but two or three half-generations is not an improbable period to assign. The change that we seek must be very deep-rooted and very far-reaching. Such changes usually require a full generation for even the most capable to digest, and another full generation for the group to embody them into institutional forms. Fortunately for progress, continued insecurity and lack of opportunity will reinforce study, probably for the majority. We must study in season and out. Our immediate reliance must be on free and full discussion, for we honestly seek the best things for all concerned. In the long run the people themselves must decide. Our ultimate reliance is on the pursuit of intelligence. There is no other firm foundation.

Such is our situation. It is yet night, but not so dark that we cannot work.

IV

DEMOCRACY AND RESPECT
FOR PERSONALITY*

DEMOCRACY began in history as a government of the people, the protest of the many against the one-sided and selfish rule of one man, or of a favored few, over the rest. It seemed then, and history appears to corroborate it, that no one man, nor any prior-chosen few, can be trusted with arbitrary rule over the rest. Any scheme of self-sufficient authority inevitably degenerates into tyranny. It is this fact which, in spite of many repeated efforts to the contrary, underlies the perennial urge to democracy. Arbitrary rule becomes in time tyrannical, and informed human personality always, sooner or later, rejects tyranny.

It is the consideration of such problems as the foregoing that has carried the conception of democracy beyond mere government. Sufficiently considered, the study of democracy brings us into society itself, into a study of associated living and how this should be managed that men may together live best.

But living together leads straight to ethics and the proper relationship of one man to others. Long before conscious democracy in any broader sense could develop, man did much thinking on the ethical problem. It was perhaps the Egyptians who first conceived of justice as

* From *Progressive Education*, February, 1939.

applying to men as men, and not differently to higher class and lower class. *The Book of the Dead* is stern in exacting an equal justice of all alike to all alike. Christianity, coming much later, founded itself on both Egyptian and Greek achievements, stressing the sanctity of the individuals as such, with special emphasis on the good intents of the heart. The Middle Ages institutionalized all these, but not in a form that remained permanent. The Renaissance renewed emphasis on the goodness of life itself, seeing this especially as individual and personal, and recognizing particularly the goodness of a cultivated content of life. The Reformation brought stress on the sanctity of individual conscience and so eventually—perhaps unwittingly and unintentionally— brought man freedom of thinking even to the degree of questioning prior-established institutions. Modern science gave man a new faith in himself and so expanded and implemented the rising significance of individuality, with a still greater stress on freedom of thinking.

On these foundations a new and broader democracy emerged, including government but reaching beyond it, or beneath it, into the very foundations of life and relationships. This broader democracy included such elements as the following: A just ethics will wish the same good for all alike, irrespective of birth or fortune. Life is itself a good, and is so to be sought, not something to be shunned or avoided or reduced or starved; and the criteria for judging are to be found within life itself, in the shareable situations of life, where the recognized better are used for criticizing the worse in the hope of finding in the process still better criteria. The fundamental authority in all this is an intelligence built out of such socially criticized experience. Democratic social arrangements will particularly stress equality of opportunity. Education is here the great resource. It exists to help individuals grow, grow alike in this richness of being, in this socially built intelligence, and in the will to shape life on the ethical bases of equal justice and equal opportunity. Democratic government exists to foster such living for all together. And in every human association all concerned with the results of any policy shall share as far as humanly feasible in making the policy.

Freedom has been offered as a natural and inalienable right, and in the past many who spoke for democracy have accepted the claim. The criterion laid down above enables us at once to set proper bounds to freedom. It is true that democracy stresses freedom, but the freedom that it defends is a freedom that fits with a like freedom simultaneously exercised by all others concerned. No man's freedom should hurt others. But even more positively, we owe duties as truly as we exercise rights. Democracy demands of us not simply that we do not hurt, but more than this, that we actively seek such procedures and approve such policies as promise positively to help the group as a whole to go forward. These considerations of positive help have critical bearing in these modern days of all-inclusive economic interdependence. Democratic freedom is thus no excuse for selfishness. Instead, it is the strict correlative of the common good. Anything that fails to help this best we are not free to do.

The same criterion thus used for judging institutions and rights extends also to defining the proper use of all human and natural resources.   In certain parts of the world the mountains, once wooded, now stand bare and empty.   Not only are forests gone, but the soil has been washed away.   Those who thus stripped the land may have lived somewhat better for what they thus took, but they acted wrongly.   In doing as they did, they unjustly deprived their descendants and others who might come after them of forests and soil.   They refused, in effect, to include the unborn in their decisions.   Those who are to come after us have rights that we who live now are ethically bound to respect.   Our use in this country of forest and soil is herein called in question.   Our practice of almost-absolute private property rights cannot be democratically defended.   As we think of these things, it becomes exceedingly doubtful that private ownership of natural resources is justifiable.   Democracy cuts deeper and extends farther than many have been willing to admit.   On no other basis can we have adequate respect for personality.   Selfishness and democracy are mutual exclusives as regards respect for personality.

Let us now examine more closely what is involved in a proper respect for personality.   The exercise of purpose is here crucial.   To form purposes and act upon them is inherent in the desirable life.   Plato defined a slave as one who accepts his purposes from another whom we call his master.   For Plato the essence of slavery lay in separating the forming of purposes from the execution of purposes and lodging the two in separate persons.   And the distinction is capital.   We may broaden what has just been said.   The life good to live is one of acting on thinking.   To act without thinking is to act unwisely and often

unjustly.   It is not right.   One should not only think before he acts—thus improving his action—he should after
acting criticize the results.   In this way his thinking
next time may be better and consequently also his next
acting.   These things are obvious inherents of any life
worth living.

We can go further.   Just as with purposing, so should
thinking be joined with acting in the same person.   Any
régime of living which so separates thinking and acting
that they cannot and do not most intimately correct and
improve each other as discussed above—any such régime
is undemocratic.   Respect for personality demands that
thinking and acting be normally joined together within
the same person.   Otherwise, there results some form and
degree of slavery.

And in this also democracy cuts deeper and demands
more than many are willing to admit.   The management
of educational institutions and systems illustrates the
evils here possible.   There can be no effectual respect
for personality except as each one is allowed to develop
into the best that he may become.   This equality of opportunity stands perhaps closest of all things to the very
heart of democracy.   Acting on thinking is even more
educative than was brought out above.   On that as a
basis the responsible self is best built.   Only as one acts
thus, holding oneself responsible for actual consequences,
does one adequately build a responsible moral character
one that is both sensitive and intelligent as it faces life.
But in how many institutions of higher learning do presi-
dent and trustees separate to themselves the thinking that
makes policies and leave it to the instructors and other

underlings simply to carry out instructions? How many school systems are run on the "line and staff" theory, in which certain ones as "staff" think out both policies and procedures for handing down the "line" ultimately to the teachers? Under such managing, thought and act are separated much as in slavery. And the result is that the teachers fail of that best of all education-in-service which goes along with responsible thinking and acting. Moreover, such a régime of factory management for teachers leads almost inevitably to a like management of the pupils. When pupils live through twelve years of doing primarily as they are told—when that is the aim—they get used to separating act from thought. We need not wonder that so many citizens are indifferent to the public welfare. They have been taught not to think as to what should go on, and not to join acting with thinking. The situation is undemocratic—even more, it is immoral and tragic. We cannot expect children to learn democracy unless they live democracy.

When we thus advocate acting on thinking in a way which seems to demand that each one act on his own thinking, some will arise to question. Will not such a doctrine result in social chaos? Can we trust all people to do thinking that is fit to act on? What are laws for but to tell such people what to do? And, in particular, what about children? Can we trust them to act on their thinking? What are homes and schools for if not to think for immature children and tell them what to do?

These are old and familiar questions. They always have come forward when the proposal has been made to extend the range of democracy. Even this country was very careful in the beginning to restrict the suffrage to those who owned property.   Doubtless many "economic royalists" of today, as they read in the Gallup polls the distribution of support for the New Deal, wish those restrictions were still in force.   Like questions have always confronted those who proposed to give the young a greater range of responsibility in their upbringing.   It is the attitude of conservatism, which prefers the ills we have to those they can imagine.

For answers to such questions we have to get together in working agreement three overlapping ideas: respect for personality, "freedom of conscience," and the learning of character-building effects of responsible practice.   Respect for personality is our inclusive topic.   Let us, then, consider "freedom of conscience," and begin with its place in American history.

So far as this country can be said to have an historic religious foundation, that foundation is to be found in the conception of freedom of conscience.   When our ancestors used the term, as they often did, they meant something definite by it.   This thing that they meant—this faith in deciding each for himself what he should fundamentally believe and do, this outlook—now no longer confined to religion—has entered deeply into the soul of America.   It is almost, if not quite, the deepest article of faith in American democracy, that each man shall and of right ought to carry the final responsibility for deciding what shall be the policies to which he will give allegiance.   To the true American, this seems essential to any decent selfhood.   Without it, respect for personality can have little or no meaning.

It is interesting to trace the development of "freedom of conscience" from its early religious application to a now broader and more fundamental reach.

The first one known to give utterance to the idea was Theodoric the Ostrogoth, who said: "We cannot by edict set up a religion, for no one can be compelled to believe against his will." George Mason, author of the Virginia Declaration of Rights, James Madison, and Thomas Jefferson—all, when they faced the like issue in this country, repeated in effect the same idea, Mason perhaps first in his Virginia Declaration of Rights. Madison used almost Theodoric's own words that "religion and the manner of discharging it can be directed only by reason and conviction, not by force or violence." Thomas Jefferson gave it a slightly different turn, in his *Bill for Establishing Religious Freedom*, "The opinions and belief of men depend not on their own will, but follow involuntarily the evidence proposed to their minds."

All the earlier quotations had religion in mind as the occasion, but each looked deeper and saw that belief is something inherent in the character of the person himself. Jefferson's apt words suggest the answer to the problem raised by the conservative opponents of democracy, whether in government or in school. Belief—the belief that one acts upon—resides not simply in the person. He cannot arbitrarily choose whether he shall or shall not believe; he will follow the evidence as he sees it. Nor does belief reside simply in the thing itself —we no longer even speak of self-evident truths. No; belief resides neither in the person alone nor in the thing alone, but in both, in both in the way this thing appeals to me.

Freedom of conscience in the wider view is, then, simply accepting these facts as to how men do believe and using them as the basis of democratic decision and responsibility. But we can do this wisely only as we bring simultaneously to bear on this the third of the ideas named above—the learning or character-building effects of responsible practice.

The critics of democracy, pointing to the common people in their present state of ignorance, indifference, and prejudice, have called to high heaven that such people are not fit to make responsible decisions of policy. The critics of democratic educative processes have similarly stressed the ignorance, short-sightedness, and emotionality of children, and have urged therefore the unwisdom of trusting any decisions to them. Such critics overlook two things: first, that common people (any people anywhere) and children are quite able to reason with a high degree of reliability about things that really concern them. Their reasoning is in itself likely to be good, their weakness (where it exists) is largely in a present lack of knowledge and range of informed concern. They have the ability; they lack experience. Secondly, these critics overlook the capital fact that the way for either group to learn is to start practising with what they now have. Working on their own concerns, which they will be serious about, they will find both reason and opportunity to take more into account in order to serve their own interests. Thus growth ensues, growth along the line where weakness had before existed.

In other words, our historic freedom of conscience, properly expanded, becomes alike the key to a democratic respect for personality and to a democratic system of education lying inherent in life. In still other words, democracy wisely used contains within itself the means of its own correction.

The last statement leads to the final point—and an important one it is. We who direct education, whether informally by public criticism or more formally in the schools, must consciously uphold the ideal implicit in the foregoing discussion. I, being the kind of person that I am, believe what appeals to me. This is true, but believability is not therefore simply personal and private. Far from it. I cannot and should not simply follow personal whims as I decide what to think and do. We are, as any adequate study of the self will show, inherently and inextricably social, social both in origin and in outlook. We must act socially; we cannot live otherwise. We need, then, to think those things that allow us to work together co-operatively with other people. Science builds its objectivity on this principle. If no one else can see what I think I see, there is something wrong somewhere, and presumably with me. I have to convince other competent observers. So I must make the rule of my acceptance of facts or ideas that they be the kind that competent observers coming after me will corroborate. I may appeal to the future as against present prejudice, but even so I am appealing to the future competents. I am not simply believing of "my own sweet will."

We then who would educate must help to build this

ideal criterion of what to accept in fact and practice. Such a criterion respects me for all I am worth, but no further.   It makes the most exacting possible demands of me while it respects me and my stand, as far as they will stand criticism, ultimate competent criticism.   This is what I take John Dewey to mean when he says that, "Intelligence after millions of years of errancy has found itself as a method. . . ." We begin by respecting each person, respecting him, however, not simply as he is but even more with respect to what he may become.   We respect him as he is by letting him start now, with his present shortcomings, but also with his present promises. But we demand of him as we demand of ourselves that he accept to act on only those ideas that will bear criticism. This brings in the social factor, which is the essence of reliable intelligence.   We apply, each to himself, as best he can learn to do, the most competent conceivable criticism.   The rest of us help by criticizing.   This is the method of discussion, the method of democracy. Thus is our historic freedom of conscience brought up to date.   This is true respect for personality.

V

THE TEACHER'S PLACE IN THE SOCIAL LIFE OF TODAY*

A T NO other time in our history has the proper work of the teacher been so much in dispute among us as today. In any clear-cut social-political theory of a country, the place assigned to the teacher is in conformity with that theory. In the totalitarian states accordingly, the teacher, whether in the lower or in the higher schools, is the propagandist agent of the state to inculcate its authoritarian social-political creed to the rising generation. In this country, just what part the teacher ought to take in social life and change is much in dispute, more obviously because we are engaged in remaking our social-economic-political outlook and have as yet reached no unanimity of position, less obviously because we are just now shifting our thinking in the matter of change from a position of no-change in fundamentals to a position that makes change an essential factor in all human affairs.

We accordingly find the American mind much puzzled. Shall we or shall we not provide for conscious change? Shall we or shall we not expect the school to play a significant part in helping the country to make up its mind on our disputed social-economic development? Many are the answers and variations of answers returned. At one extreme are those who say that the elementary

* *School and Society,* July 31, 1937.

and secondary school teachers must avoid all controversial issues.   This of course would mean, and often
does mean, the virtual if not the conscious indoctrination
of youth in the *status quo* outlook.   At the other extreme
are those who seem to demand that teachers shall decide among themselves on a proper reconstruction of
our social order and proceed by indoctrination to bring
up a rising generation exactly committed to that chosen
scheme.   Both these extremes agree in one thing that
this paper will reject: namely, that the school is to indoctrinate the young by fixing each its plan irrevocably
in their minds and hearts.   Each group means to train
up the young in the way they should go so that when
they are old they will not depart therefrom.

It was, I hope, not necessary to say that this paper will
agree with neither of these extremes.   The fundamental
position herein taken is that of conscious and intelligent
democracy based on the certainty of change and development, on the conscious precariousness of the future
outcome.   Changes will come.   As they come, it is our
business to steer them intelligently.   Democracy demands
that the people decide, not the present people—still less
the past—for the future, but the future people for themselves.   It is the duty, then, of the present generation
not to tell the rising generation the answers to their
social problems—we could not if we would—but to make
the rising generation as intelligent as we can in social-
political matters and leave them free to solve their own
problems.

Along with this principal dispute as to what kind of
classroom teaching we should have, there goes the fur-

ther question of the teacher's place both as a citizen of the community and as a member of one of the important learned professions having public duties outside the classroom. It may be well to take these as three questions and discuss them in the ascending order of complexity, beginning first then with the teacher's place as citizen and closing with a consideration of the teacher's proper work in the classroom.

The teacher is a citizen and as such has all the rights of other citizens. These rights include the teacher's right to live his own life as to him (or her) shall seem good, in particular to ally himself with the political party of his choice and to advocate its principles publicly. But rights are never absolute. As Bishop Brooks said, no one has a right to all his rights. Or more precisely, each right is limited—or better, constituted—by the way it works out, that is, by its consequences to all concerned when it is put into operation. This, at least as I conceive it, gives us the sole grounds for claiming any right: namely, that it works best for the highest attainable welfare of all concerned. From these considerations it follows at once that the teacher's rights as citizen and as man, or woman, in the community are limited by his duties as teacher.

Just what shall we then conclude? It seems clear that there can be no specific conclusion apart from a knowledge of the specific situation, and even then we can rely only on probability. As a rule, however, the teacher's primary duty will be to those whom he is to teach. Most, for example, would admit without question that a teacher who is openly and flagrantly immoral sets such a bad example to youth that he should accordingly be removed from his teaching post, and this even though as citizen he may in his immorality have broken no law of the state and accordingly had a legal right to be thus immoral. In social and political matters the good teacher will be sensitive to the influence his outside advocacy and conduct are having on his pupils, that this influence may be the best possible. In particular as regards his advocacy of this or that side of any controversial issue, he will wish so to conduct himself as citizen that his pupils or students shall by his example be led to think both widely and wisely, each for himself, about the issue involved. What the teacher says outside and how he speaks and acts should thus all be done with due regard not only to the social issue at stake but also to the educative effect of his acts on those under his care.

This does not mean that the teacher is not to stir up his pupils to feel and question. That may be exactly the best thing he can do for them, even if many parents and citizens prefer to have no questions raised regarding the *status quo*. It is no evil to stir them either to feel or to question; the evil to be feared is that they will answer the questions so raised without adequate study. What the teacher must do is to help his pupils to fair-minded study. If this be safeguarded, the stirring is probably all to the good.

But the teacher has wider educative effects than on his pupils. He or she is a member of the community. Within reason, the teacher should accept responsibility to share with others in helping the community study its varied social problems. The positive duty we postpone for the moment. But there is a negative duty here to be considered. If the teacher is to help parents and other citizens think more broadly, he will hardly begin by making them angry. His ideas may be more advanced and more valid, but he will as a rule secure a better study of his advanced ideas by taking pains to write and speak and act with obvious fairmindedness. Otherwise he may hurt his cause and bring the profession into contempt.

These words of caution, however, do not mean that no teacher shall ever take a stand to which others may object. Such occasions do come, and men and women of integrity will not fail to face them bravely. And the teaching profession, as will be said in a moment, should be so organized as to extend to those who thus stand proper support as it may be needed. Indeed, there may come times when one must withstand a whole community even to the extent of personal martyrdom. Such a devotion to a sufficient cause may be the highest duty. By common consent, Socrates faced such a situation and served all subsequent mankind by drinking the hemlock. By and large, however, greater service is more often done by wise tact than by headlong martyrdom.

The teacher's proper place in the community manifestly involves more problems than we have space to consider. One further thing, however, should perhaps not go unsaid. Many school systems deny to women teachers the right to marry. Some of the arguments urged in behalf of such a policy we can understand and even sympathize with, but, taking all things together, thus to deny to much more than half our teachers, just because they happen to be women, so important a part of healthy normal life seems quite indefensible. If the proposal were made to treat men so, the outraged cry of indignation would shake the very heavens. It would be an unwarrantable interference with the just rights of citizens. And so it would be, and so it is—to male or female—an immoral encroachment on life itself.

We may now pass on to the teacher as a member of a learned profession. Each profession, simply because it is such, owes public duties beyond the immediate practice of the profession. This wider duty of the teaching profession includes responsibility for helping the public to see and understand any educative effects from any part of life that significantly concern the public welfare. Research and publication are generally admitted to be proper functions of the profession, but the social significance of such is not always appreciated. We frequently wax eloquent over the cultural resources of our country, but the greatest of these resources are as yet untouched. They lie in the future, to be dug therefrom only by study and discovery and invention. Electricity is one such resource that has thus been given to us by such study in very recent times. A like instance was the study that led up to and made possible the constitution of 1787, though this is less often so considered. In the twenty-five years preceding 1787 our people built the needed social intelligence, building to be sure on the foundation already laid in British history. Right now, it seems fair to assert, we stand most in need of an analogous step forward, this time into the social-economic-political field. Problems as difficult as they are crucial confront us in the economic realm. How to solve them democratically we do not know. The 1787 situation was met largely by landed country gentlemen who had the leisure to study and the will to do it. The modern counterpart is largely, though not entirely, the university professor.

They and all other members of our profession must accept responsibility to bring effectively before the public, for example, such evil educative factors as the slums, where criminals are mostly bred. It is not ours to clear out the slums, but it is ours to help the public see the need for getting rid of them. Similarly for the malnutrition of the young, whether due to ignorance or to poverty. The state must deal adequately with it, and we must help the state to see the need. So also with inequality of educational opportunity, that the poor and certain racial groups are in effect denied the democratic opportunity in comparison with others of becoming what God or nature made them capable of being. And the evil effects of competition for profits and the disastrous moral and cultural results therefrom within our civilization. We must somehow get everybody to see the true facts of our divided culture. As a great man has said, "If ever there was a house of civilization divided within itself and against itself, it is ours today."

All these evils it is the public duty of professional educators to understand—for the evils are educative effects, mis-educative effects that hurt and lower life. Because they are educative effects, it becomes our peculiar duty to study them and let others see and understand the public damage thus done. We can not ourselves remedy the evils, but we are peculiarly responsible for pointing them out, and—if I may anticipate—for bringing up a generation both sensitive to what is involved and intelligent to deal with the situation.

As we consider the teaching profession, its right and duty to organize come forward as an urgent problem. That teachers should have the right to form such professional organizations as to them seem good would appear to be a democratic axiom. Here and there over the country, however, are school systems that forbid teachers to join the Teachers' Union, partly, some say, because it is affiliated with the American Federation of Labor. As I do not myself belong to the Teachers' Union and am critical of certain acts that have at times emanated from it, I feel free to speak my mind on this point. I see nothing but gross injustice and dangerous oppression in denying teachers the right to join the Union. Surely, teachers have the same right as other citizens to form organizations as they deem best in behalf of their professional purposes.

Whether teachers should permanently ally themselves with any non-educational body or movement I am frank to say I feel doubtful. Any individual educator or body of educators has that right, I claim it for them; but I doubt the wisdom of educators as such committing themselves to permanent alliance with any but an educational body devoted to educational ends and using only educational methods. Educational organizations, it would seem, are by that fact educationally limited as to the ends they will pursue and the methods they will use. The proper bounds are easier to conceive in general than to state with preeision. Educators as such are, as was said earlier, primarily responsible for educative effects. They have clearly the right to seek conditions favorable to proper educative effects, a decent wage, participation of teachers in determining educational policies, proper tenure laws, adequate freedom in teaching. They have also the right to seek those more indirect but still necessary conditions that in fact affect educative results: for example, a better tax system in order that there may be more school support, a better school law in order that there may be better schools, a bond issue that rightly concerns educational welfare. In all these there is, to be sure, danger that mere selfish purposes may become dominant, and educators should be keenly sensitive to the danger. For teachers to become simply one more pressure group organized principally for selfish advantages—this I hope we may never see.

The final of our three questions is probably the one that interests us most. What are the rights and duties of teachers in respect of dealing with current controversial issues along social, economic, and political lines? Or, perhaps more precisely, what, if any, proper part has the school in the conscious effort to effect social change?

To shorten the discussion, let me say outright that for my part I reject all high-Marxism with its dialectic materialism, including its class-struggle conception and tactics. Also I reject any resort to "indoctrination" or use of the school for "propaganda" purposes. The situation confronting us, as I see it, is that sketched at the outset. The development of modern science and its application to invention and technology have brought into modern industrial society a crucial new characteristic: namely, the fact of inclusive economic interdependence; the depression proved it to the hilt. We were all involved. Another new characteristic of our modern industrial society is the fact that now, for the first time in history, it is possible to create enough wealth for an economy of plenty. We could, if we only would, all live in comfort.

How to effect such comfort on a democratic basis is to be worked out, I judge, in the next three half-generations. Whether we shall fail and give up democracy for some sort of totalitarian state is in the lap of the gods. Our best hope to prevent this (and I believe it can suffice) is to set to work and build a social intelligence adequate to solve the problem. Our success in building scientific intelligence within recent times gives us valid grounds for hope. I cannot take the time to argue it, but I assure you that social intelligence can be built, and, within limits, to order, if only we will bring to the task the intelligence we now have.

The work of the school to this end is, I think, clearly defined: namely, to build before adulthood useful social ideals, habits of democratic study and action, and actual social intelligence. These three aims are overlapping and inter-penetrative. To accomplish these ends the school will work along two main lines: first, that of socially useful activities, preferably co-operative community activities; and secondly, the study of live social issues, many of which will be controversial in character. Through the co-operative community activities the pupils will act on social thinking and therein build social habits and attitudes along with social intelligence.

Through the treatment of live and controversial issues we shall build social intelligence.

The problem of controversial issues demands our closest consideration. Let us distinguish several kinds and degrees. First, are certain *once-were* controversial matters, but now no longer so, such as the Copernican system of astronomy, geology, and evolution (in scientific circles). Second, are *elsewhere-controversial* questions, such as democracy and freedom of speech and press in the totalitarian states. (These are often in fact still controversial with us, though professedly they have long been settled.) Third, are certain *locally-controversial* issues, such as evolution in Tennessee (or parts thereof) and in many other regions. Fourth, are certain highly dangerous controversial questions, such as any proposal to change marriage or religion. Fifth, are certain dangerous but still necessary controversial problems, such as those now relating to labor and capital and economic affairs in general.

The school will treat these five groups differently. We shall teach the *once-were* and *elsewhere* controversial without special question, only taking pains to make our young people intelligent in their use and especially to be intelligently able to effect such changes in our present conceptions of them as the now unknown future developments may later demand. This is, of course, the very opposite of indoctrination. With regard to the highly dangerous questions, the lowest school will mostly avoid them, the high school will treat them very carefully, according to circumstances; but the college and university must be free to consider them without restraint. With regard to *locally* controversial and the *dangerous-but-necessary* questions the schools will walk warily, knowing the sensitivities of people, but none the less must use every reasonable endeavor to make all our young people —and old ones, too, if they can—so intelligent regarding them that the needed reconstruction of conception and institution in these areas can go on wisely and adequately. Let it be clear that what the teacher should aim at with his pupils is not converts to some previously chosen schemes but their own intelligent self-direction.

In respect of these difficult but necessary controversial issues the profession and the public should be clear. We cannot afford not to make our young people intelligent regarding them, as critically intelligent as we can. Anything else is a suicidal public policy. And we must not wait till the young people are grown. We must educate before the mind is grown and finished, built for all time and fixed by the cares of this world and the deceitfulness of riches as we see today in too many of the selfishly rich among us. And the profession must organize to protect the individual teacher in the just discharge of his duty here. Reasonable discussion of all pertinent controversial issues is absolutely necessary to intelligent citizenship. In this matter democracy depends on the school. We must not fail. The free play of intelligence is society's only permanent hope.

VI

IMPLICATIONS OF ADULT
EDUCATION FOR A DEMOCRACY*

W HY does democracy need adult education? What
can adult education do for democracy? These are
the two questions that I am going to discuss.

First, let us try to clear up what I mean by adult education. I mean by adult education any conventionalized,
directed, connected education that is carried on by adults
or older adolescents and is not a part of a regular school
program. I'd like to think, especially for the purpose
that I have in mind, of groups of citizens working on
problems of citizenship. Of course there is a great deal
more to adult education than that, but when I speak of
its meaning for democracy that is the most significant
part, although there are other parts of lesser practicality
for the present lesson. Emphatically, I mean any kind of
study that enhances life; more emphatically, I mean the
social, economic, and political problems.

We have noted in an earlier chapter that democracy
includes, first, a dominating regard for human personality and, secondly, the final control of all institutions
by the people. The people, by themselves, are to make
any changes they see fit. They, however, are under moral
obligation, as they build our institutions and as they

* Stenographic report of a talk before the Adult Education Council
of Chicago.

change them, to take account of what I just said about respecting personality. That is to say, no tyranny of the majority shall be imposed on a minority. A majority, just because it is a majority, has no right to ride rough-shod over a minority. The majority is under moral obligation to consider the minority and at all times to develop expression of human personality, all on a sub-stantially equal basis.

Our problem is the implication of adult education for democracy. What is wrong with democracy? Why bother with it? There is, I believe, nothing fundamentally wrong with our idea of democracy. The only difficulty is that we haven't enough of it. We need more democ-racy. We have had a rather poor imitation of democracy. We need a thorough one. In that sense there is nothing the matter with democracy except that we haven't given it a chance. But our actual democracy does suffer, and it suffers from what I am going to call the culture.

Let me talk about that a little to show what I mean by culture. By culture, I mean everything—language and customs and standards and ideals and tools and imple-ments and instrumentalities—that man has discovered or devised by means of which we live together.

On the material side, take, for instance, a desk, a table. A man thought them up, learned how to make them, did make them. He added them to our accumulating ma-terial culture. But there is also a human side of such things—the use of them, how to make them, how to deal with them. Children, as they come on, have to learn how to use them. Each rising generation has to learn about such things. That is part of the culture. In the last fifty years the electric light has become a part of culture. Electricity has been here all the time, but we didn't know how to use it. It was present only in lightning so far as we knew. It is only in the last fifty years that we have learned how to use it, and it has produced light for us. That is part of culture—how to make it, how to use it. So the culture consists of all the things that man has learned and thought through which we live. Maybe you want to call it communicable knowledge embodied in the form of the instrumentalities of life.

The young come into a world in which culture is already in operation. They have to live in that group. They are taken care of by their parents. As they get older, they gradually fit into the life of their parents, the life they became acquainted with in their group while growing up. They have to acquire culture in order to live. They have to learn the language to live, to use their clothes in order to live decently, to learn to eat food. Eventually they have to learn how to use knives and forks, cups and saucers. They have to learn how to get along with people. They are acquiring culture as they learn more and more how to live the lives of the group in which they grow up.

In my opinion, it is culture that makes one group of people different from another. If you go to France you find that the French behave somewhat differently from the Germans. It is the culture. It isn't anything innate in the French that makes them different from the Germans. My opinion is that if we had some way of changing one hundred thousand French children for one hundred thousand German children, except that they might look a little different on the outside, nobody would know they were changed. Those born on the other side of the Rhine would think the same as those born on this side, and vice versa. You could not tell the difference.

This notion of race is absolutely fraudulent. Chinese, Caucasians, and Negroes are essentially the same. In my opinion, there is no difference in ability and no difference in taste, aptitude, or any of those things, so far as birth goes. It is culture that makes people, and it is by means of, and through, the culture that we live.

If culture is going to be so necessary to our living and if it is in and through culture that we live, then the culture has to be balanced and one part of it fitted with another part. If you find a civilization that is in good working order, that civilization has a culture in which one part exactly dovetails into each other part, so that they work harmoniously to produce the good life for those people.

Many older civilizations have shown this to a great degree. Take China. Up to a hundred years ago western civilization had no influence over the Chinese. They had a culture then, which was old, very articulate, and high grade in comparison with the western world; a culture that fitted, part with part, to an astonishing degree. This had a tremendous effect on the people that were born into it. It took them as babes and brought them up in this culture, and to those that lived that way, it was the only way. One part fitted to another. Life went on smoothly, evenly, with very little conflict.

But now the western culture has begun to come in and upset the balance over there. China is having great trouble. The reason for this war is that China has not yet consistently remade its culture after western impact. That is, it is part western and part old; the parts don't fit together. In new China they need a unified social outlook. China has great difficulty in getting together, in uniting, and it is that fact which has aroused the Japanese to come in as they have. The Chinese have to learn to unite, to co-operate. They don't know how to do it, but they are learning fast.

Our own culture, up to a hundred years ago, was fairly unified, articulated, fitted one part with another; but in this country, in the last one hundred years, a new factor has come to upset this balance. We have become industrialized. A hundred years ago most of the people lived on farms, and were relatively self-sufficient. They raised food and made on the farm nearly everything they used, sold a little of it to the trader near by and bought from him the little they needed to buy. Each farm was relatively independent; and we had a pretty balanced life on this basis.

But when the industrial situation came, it upset this balance. We have learned now how to build, how to manufacture, how to produce to a far greater degree than ever before; and we do produce a great deal more. Many people have great wealth because of modern machine arrangements. The factories employ a great many men. But it is the production side of our culture that has changed; and the distribution side has remained very much as it was.

We still need more change. Production has increased very rapidly, but the means of distributing the products are very much the same as they were; and these two things don't fit. For example, one tenth of one per cent of families at the top have as much as the 42 per cent at the bottom. That is disproportionate.

We are in doubt as to what to do morally. The culture is upset. It is uneven, not fitted together; and, since it doesn't fit together, it creates social problems.

It is right there that we have our dangers. Some people who own property profit by certain arrangements as they now prevail. They got their property under those arrangements and they like to hold their property; they, therefore, do not wish the culture to be changed in respect to their privileges.

The culture must be articulate, must be well-balanced. If, for any reason, it is not well-balanced, there is strain and difficulty. Those who profit by older ways are much opposed to changing it to get the thing once more in balance; and this is the basis of our present social, economic, and political disputes. It profits some people to keep it unbalanced, and it would profit more people if it were balanced—there is the dispute.

The danger is that those who don't see and understand these changes will sit on the lid until there is too much steam accumulated and the lid will get blown off. The danger is that those who profit by the present arrangements and those who, because of inertia, are unwilling to have the culture brought back into balance by bringing up the rear of it, will be able to prevent change long enough to make the problems worse and create great social strain.

There democracy becomes involved. Certain gov-

ernments in Europe that were more or less democratic
now have dictators. Why? They were not able to solve
their problems on a democratic basis. If you look closely
at them, you will observe that they are countries that
more recently adopted the democratic, parliamentary
system of government. They did not have enough experience with it as England or this country had had; and,
with their limited experience in democracy, were not
able to make it work. When they faced social difficulties
and could not solve them, they changed from democracies to dictatorships. It was a failure of unskilful democracy to solve the difficult problems of the modern
mind.

Let's say it like this: Science and invention are increasing in a geometrical ratio. It is the scientific side
of our culture that is growing the most rapidly. If science
and invention and technology continue to increase more
rapidly than the other parts, strains will increase, problems will increase, and if they increase beyond a certain
amount, social catastrophe will come. That means dictatorship. That is what happened to those countries in
Europe.

This, then, is the danger point: that one part of the
culture rushes ahead and one part lags behind, and some
people don't see that if they put the brake on and keep
the lagging parts still more lagging instead of trying to
bring them up, it means catastrophe. I am not advocating at the present time any particular change. I am
saying that the culture has got to be reasonably in balance. If it gets more and more out of balance, then we
are heading for trouble.

The way to save democracy is to get more people to study our problems and find out what is wrong in order to change it before it is too late. If we don't do that, we will get social catastrophe and dictatorship. If we do do that, democracy will solve the problems in some fashion.

I am not at all interested, at the present time, in holding up any solution, in advocating anything; so let us see where the problem lies. We may say it like this: There are two great needs of our times which go together. In order to achieve a balanced culture we need, first, minds that are plastic, open to argument, able and willing to study and to follow the argument where the study shall lead; and, secondly, we need the determination to put into operation what the study indicates.

How are we going to do it?   How are we going to get these two things?   As I see the situation, there are three answers in the world today.   There is the fascist answer; there is the dialectical materialism answer; and there is the democratic answer.

The fascist answer runs somewhat like this: **Here is** a country that doesn't know its own mind.   It is more or less in chaos.   The fascist answer is that a leader (such as Mussolini) comes forward and gets control.   He may get control by some kind of governmental voting, or he may seize control; but he gets control.

That doesn't bring unity—yet.   But he has control. He then proceeds, by steps, to seize the newspapers, the radio, and the other organs of communication.   With them he sets out to build the minds of his people by telling them what they are to think, but letting them know only what he wishes them to hear, by keeping out news that he doesn't want to have put in the newspapers. He tells them what to think and how to think, and (this is the crux of the matter) makes the schools an indoctrination agency. The schools tell the children what to think, bring them up believing what the dictator wishes them to believe. By means of propaganda and indoctrination, the dictator builds the minds of the people to his model.

That is the fascist way. You can see it in Italy and Germany. People are not encouraged to think—not for themselves. You can't keep people from thinking somewhat, but they are told what the news is and they are told what to think. By one way and another the dictator hopes to build the people to his mind and bring them to think his way. Then he tells them what they are supposed to do.

The Marxian dialectical materialism is somewhat different. It is at once a philosophy and a program of action. I said Marxian. I am not sure that Marx held just the same ideas that some people proclaim in his name. I call it "high Marxian." What is dialectical materialism? It is this: that at any one time the country is likely to go too far in reaction, with two opposed factions pitted against each other. They will come together and then there will be a forward move. In our times, capitalism is in control. Those who own will exploit those who do not own. They will go too far in their exploiting, grind people down. The exploited will resent it and they will react. When they have reacted enough (when enough of them get angry), they will rise and dispossess the capitalist class and then you have a dictatorship of the proletariat, a forward move of a class to a classless society.

It is a program in that those who believe in adopting this program will encourage the capitalistic crowd and then encourage the people to get angry with the capitalistic crowd, stir up the capitalists to do more violent things, and then stir up the proletariat to get angry and go the other way.   They work on both to make the conflicts greater.   That they call "class struggle," and they hope that out of the class struggle will come revolution and the dictatorship of the proletariat.

Those who think they see the furthest, hold the light in their hands and try to lead the others.   They are willing to indoctrinate their children; they are willing to use their program today; they are willing to increase the class struggle on both sides so as to get the revolution over quickly—the sooner the better—they are willing not to use democratic processes to bring it about.   They say that ultimately we shall have a democracy, but they are not willing to use democratic processes in bringing it about.

Now, the third means of getting this thing done is the democratic way, which says that we are not to say in advance in an authoritative way what people should think but to argue it out.   We are to get people intelligent about the situation in order that they may think intelligently—in order that intelligence may rule.   That is our aim.

We may have a double aim, which is not inconsistent. For example, as a citizen I may believe that the country should adopt such and such policies; as a teacher I am mainly concerned with developing intelligence in those with whom I work, not mainly concerned that they believe my doctrines, but that they become intelligent about the situation. If I do honestly believe in democracy and mean to work consistently for it, I'll not use my position to indoctrinate those under me. I'll not use my possibilities for propaganda (in the narrow and bad sense of propaganda today); but I'll use my educational opportunities in the effort to make each person that I deal with more ably independent in his own field.

Democracy, then, has as its program to make each person capably independent and intelligent in his own thinking, with the understanding that it is going to trust those people to do their own thinking in their own good time. We who believe in democracy would set to work to make our people intelligently independent; and that would make them able to judge us.

Let's go back and see the fascist method, the high Marxian method, and this democratic principle. In fascism it is the leader (Mussolini or Hitler) and a coterie of his choice who do all the thinking. They tell the people what to think, and by a program of indoctrination, they make the people accept it. But the people never have an independent chance to think it through, and they are not allowed any individual voice in decisions. They are used, kept in relative ignorance, told what to think and what to think about, and what the facts are—but the decisions are made by the leader. The ruler is the only one who thinks, and the other people are made to think what he thinks.

The dialectical materialists have a program. Those who belong to the Party have fixed in advance what is going to happen. They know it and they believe it has to happen that way.   They have a certain fatalism.   It has to be that way.   It can't be any other way.   They can help it along.   But they have no intention of getting people to the place where they are intelligent enough to make another kind of decision as to what shall happen. It has to come out one way.   They, therefore, use propaganda and indoctrination to get more people to see the way they see.   The crowd that does the leading does the thinking, and brings the other people to their way of thinking.

In democracy it is the other way about.   We do literally believe, if we believe in democracy, that we have to make people intelligently independent.   We use all of our freedom of speech and freedom of press.   We use a kind of teaching in elementary and secondary, higher, and adult education that makes each person more and more intelligently independent.

Adult education has a peculiar power.   We haven't nearly enough adult education, in my judgment.   We ought to have every citizen in this country in more or less definite, conscious connection with study groups.   We have to have an enormous expansion of adult education, because, to go back to the situation facing us, we have many unsolved problems at the present time that may be increasing rather rapidly.   The problems outrun the solutions.   This will remain true if the reactionaries have their way and prevent people from becoming intelligent regarding the situation.   There is bound to be trouble if they have their way and it will end in social catastrophe and violent revolution.

The antidote for violent revolution is wide-spread

education of the people, all the people, in order that they may become intelligent, that they may solve the problems, that out of their intelligent study they may make up the answers. Nobody picks out the answers in advance. By their study they pick them out.

It is my business in life to discuss education: elementary, secondary, higher, and adult. We have a difference of opinion among educators as to how to run education. There are those who think (it used to be the prevailing notion) that the school was to pick certain ideals and teach them. That is the same as dictatorship or the Russian state. On this basis, the ideas that the children and young people have to learn are chosen in advance. That is anti-democratic. I am ashamed to say it, but it is probably true that, if you were to ask most people, they would still answer that the schools should do that sort of thing. In exactly the same way, they think of adult education by means of books and lectures and so on. Somehow, the ones teaching should tell those other people what to think.

I myself wish to take exactly the contrary attitude. It is our business as teachers of young people to bring them to the place where they can, and will, do their own thinking and work out a program of policies as they go along.

If I had any guess, it would be that, beginning with 1929, it will take three half-generations to solve our social, economic, and political problems. The crux of it is economic. We are going forward and backward. The generation at present in control, the New Dealers, will go a certain way. There will come a reaction. Then, in a half-generation, a new crowd, who are young now, will be the New Dealers of that day, and they will be impatient with the short steps that the present New Deal is taking. They will want longer steps, and they will understand what to do. There will be a reaction to that and there will come in the third half-generation, another crowd, impatient with them, and they will carry the thing into reasonable consistency. By that time there will be more problems to work on.

I might say a word or two about the difference between the functions of higher education, adult education, and the lower schools. It is primarily the function of higher education to do the most creative thinking, to think out and test out in a more thoroughgoing way. It is the business of the lower schools to bring up a new generation who shall be more intelligent. It is the business of adult education to take hold of the problems as they are with people (as they now are) and make people more intelligent in solving the problems that now face us (and they do face us). And we must keep on working in this way because of the new problems that arise.

Let's sum up the argument and come to adult education more precisely. Science and invention, technology, have caused and are causing increased production and all of the things that are closely connected with increased production, causing that side of our civilization to rush ahead far more rapidly than the other side. But the side that has to do with the distribution of what is produced, our conceptions as to how it should be distributed, our moral ideas, our religion, our philosophies of life—that side of life changes less rapidly.

You can always get people to adopt a better way of

doing what they wish to do. It is easy enough to get people to adopt what they wish to adopt, but very difficult to change their more fundamental modes of life. When the white man came to this country, it didn't take the Indians long to find out that the rifle could beat the bow and arrow, so the Indians very soon adopted guns and gunpowder; but they thoroughly resisted the way of living of the white people. They didn't want to change their ways of living. They wanted guns and gunpowder to carry on better their present way of living.

We are now in that same condition. We can and will make and sell more goods; we have no trouble in getting the people to believe in that. But when it comes to changing our distribution of the profits, to asking what is moral and what is not moral regarding profits, to changing the government—then we move slowly.

We are living in this country under county governments devised in the seventeenth and eighteenth centuries. Most of these governments don't fit an urban population at all. New York City has five counties. They are worthless, except to politicians who place their friends in jobs. They don't do any good at all, but the politicians hold on to them because there are that many offices to fill. Our county governments belong to the horse and buggy stage and were made when this country was predominantly agricultural. They don't fit at all, but could you get them to change? It is very, very difficult to do that.

When one part of our culture changes more rapidly than others, then strains are introduced. Strains bring their problems. If the strains become too great, problems become numberless and there has to be an explosion, as there has been in the weaker democracies and parliamentary governments.   They went over into dictatorship because they didn't have enough practice with democracy to make it work.   We are more fortunate, but there is a limit.   We cannot expect, for example, to let our problems increase indefinitely, or we, too, will reach the breaking point.   We have to get more people better able to solve our problems by the democratic process or we, too, will break.

Adult education is exactly the answer to that problem, and we need to have a great deal more of it.   We can't trust our newspapers.   There are no papers that can be trusted to give us a full discussion.

The future of democracy, then, depends on getting our people to bring the lagging parts of the culture abreast of the others.   If we ever get our culture on an even keel and if people keep it that way, there is no telling what we could do.   If, on the other hand, we allow those reactionaries who don't wish the culture changed at certain points, to have their way, then problems will accumulate and there will be a break-down.   Adult education is the answer; and it has to be very much more wide-spread and more serious than it has been.

VII

THE FUTURE OF
ADULT EDUCATION*

IT IS not prophecy, but the discussion of a desirable
policy, that constitutes the aim of this paper. When
we are clear on policy, steps can be directed intelligently.
The finding of a defensible policy is thus the first step
on the road toward intelligent action.

How shall we rank the Adult Education movement?
From time to time new and highly significant advances
appear in the development of civilization. Democratic
government may be named as one such advance. Universal tax-supported education is another. Possibly a
new economic democracy is even now arising to constitute a third. For myself, I am convinced that the Adult
Education movement of our day ought to become important enough to be included with the others as a genu-
inely significant advance in the historic development of
our civilization.

It frequently happens that when any such advance is
coming to be recognized as significant, certain ones will
seek to disparage it on the grounds that it is not really
new. We have long had efforts and activities that could
properly be called Adult Education. The assertion is
true, but the implication is false. Nothing significant
ever springs suddenly into being, and it is no disparage-

* *New York State Education,* December, 1937.

ment that any rising movement has long been present in unnamed anticipatory forms. The important thing is that a really new phase of conscious importance has been attained. This is now distinctly true of Adult Education.

That we have always had social activities and even institutions that educated out-of-school adults is clear beyond question. The New England town meeting was highly educative. The popular churches, especially where congregationally managed, have likewise had profound educative effect. Mechanics' Institutes of an earlier day and labor unions of a later day have been more precisely educative. In fact, every organization of every sort that discusses its aims and plans is to that extent educative. Political parties may thus be definitely educative. The most significantly informal educative movement in American history was the study of constitutional government that accompanied the American Revolution and culminated in the making of the Constitution. This is in fact one of the significant developments in the social-intellectual history of the world. That it was the result of wide-spread shared study seems beyond question. What we did then by a study of political democracy, we should repeat in the next generation in the realm of economic-political management, only this time the study must be more wide-spread.

So far as appears, the term Adult Education came to this country from England just after the World War. Some of us recall meeting with Mr. Mansbridge as he told us of the movement in that country. England, in our eyes, is a curious compound of caste and democracy.

Adult Education was to them an effort to even up, in a measure, the education of the underprivileged. Not all Britishers agreed with Mr. Mansbridge but it seemed fairly evident, to me at any rate, that he meant Adult Education as a kind of social opiate to make the workers better content with the station in life into which they had been born. His stress was on culture in preference to social and economic problems.

We have in this country our underprivileged also. But we are increasingly seeing that it is a state of affairs we cannot afford, and that not simply from considerations of democratic justice and equality. Illiteracy is an economic handicap not simply to the illiterates themselves, but also to our production system. The illiterate are by that very fact not as economically productive as a better education would make them. From a mere production-of-goods point of view we must raise the educational level of large numbers of our people. The cost in dollars would be more than offset by the added net income to the country at large.

The same thing is true of re-education in trade and vocation. We cannot afford to scrap workers just because their particular skill has been outmoded by a new machine. We must re-educate them vocationally, and again not simply because it is the just and decent thing to save a man's morale but because it will pay the country in the increased output of productive goods that he can still furnish. This, too, will pay in dollars and cents.

But most strategic of these possible human savings are the unemployed adolescents. These now threaten to be our most strategic waste. Unless we can somehow take adequate care of their morale and see them safely settled in jobs and married, with homes of their own—unless these things can be done, this group becomes our chief source of criminals and derelicts—a price we cannot afford to pay.   And again is the mere money cost prohibitive? To take adequate educational care of these young people, with an education that fits them, is far less expensive in dollars and cents than to let them lose self-respect and drift into crime and vice.

These demands on us to take just and proper care of the underprivileged in our midst represent what may be called remedial lines of work.   They are necessary, absolutely necessary, because of our past sins and present social shortcomings.   But we must not be content with remedial work.   It is the positive program of construction and prevention to which we must give greatest heed so as to make life finer and richer for all together.   It is this long-term program that most concerns us, an intensive program—actually inclusive of everybody.   It may be that the term Adult Education is too heavily laden with underprivileged implications to carry the burden we need to put on it.   If so, let us adopt another name. As for that I care not; it is the thing that counts, the new social program of ever-continuing inclusive education.

And why do we wish or need universal Adult Education?   The answer is clear.   There has come a new need for ever-continued thinking in the world of human affairs.   In an older day custom and recognized authority ruled, custom in ordinary details, obedience to authority in new and greater matters.   In a way that we of the modern world can hardly conceive, authority and unquestioned obedience thereto ruled among men. Politically we find this in feudalism and later in the divine right of kings. The same authority and unquestioned obedience ruled in religion, where the church or the book was the final appeal. A like authority and obedience ruled also in matters of thought. Men thought as they were told to think.

In various ways has this rule of custom and obedience been gradually broken down. The Renaissance reinstated a world of secular thought and refined enjoyment. The Reformation taught men, probably unwittingly and even unwillingly, to put individual conscience first. A new science taught men a new confidence in human thinking. Successive political revolutions in England and France united with this new science to destroy the divine right of kings, and usher in eighteenth-century liberalism and political democracy.

But custom still ruled for most people in most aspects of life. Then came the industrial revolution, with the later growth of technology and its application to large-scale production. Life has become very different, with very, very rapid changes in ways of producing, in ways of living, in ways of thinking. The sway of tradition has been broken as never before. Greater changes of attitude have come in the past hundred years than in thousands before. Probably a larger proportion of our people are now uncertain what to think about fundamentals than was ever before true of any people in all of history.

But even this is not all. The Great War shook civilization to its depths. The great depression has made our people question our economic system as never before. And the end is not yet. With science growing in geometrical ratio, there promises ever more rapid change. New problems thus arise and must, so far as we can foresee, continue to arise forever. Modern man faces as never before the continual demand to meet and solve new problems. It is a permanent new demand. And we dare not refuse it. The risk and danger otherwise would be prohibitive.

Continually new problems mean continually new study. And if democracy holds—as I for one sincerely hope it will—all must study, not simply the "leaders." Each one is a leader of some, and all must at least understand if they are to co-operate intelligently. And no twelve years of schooling, nor sixteen, nor any fixed amount, can suffice for the ever-coming new problems. All citizens must study, no matter what previous learning. We must have nothing less than universal, ever-continuing adult education.

And how widely shall we study? What problems should engage our attention? For answer we ask, How wide is life? New situations and new problems may be expected to arise in all areas of life. Without proper study any affected aspect of life is in danger of not being so good as it should be. We can draw no lines to cut off any significant part of life. Our question can only be whether the matter counts sufficiently in life.

The remedial aspects mentioned earlier we must maintain. They constitute a positive moral and democratic duty which we cannot neglect. To attend to them pays, pays socially, measured by any standard. But, in the long run, the broader and deeper study of our civilization itself is what counts most. It is the most essential. It promises the greatest returns.

Who shall pay the bills for this universal study? The support must finally come from all the wealth of all the people. There is no other way. This means, as I see it, support by public tax money, partly local, partly state, partly national, in order to even up inequalities. That the main work be tax supported and therefore publicly controlled does not deny freedom to any and all to study; there will also be volunteer organizations. But, in the long run, only public support will suffice.

How shall this inclusive system of Adult Education be managed? The fundamental principle of management must be to serve, not rule. Each local group must control itself, with the possibility of getting advice and help on support upon reasonable conditions. But there must be helpers and advisors provided at public expense, and these (not the people who study) must be managed by some scheme of shared local-state-and-national control. These helpers will stand ready to encourage study groups and forums, suggest possible lines of study with suggestive materials and sources. They will also help arrange for lecturers and guiding-helpers.

Who shall say what shall be studied? Please notice that I did not ask, What shall be *taught*? Each local class-group must be its own final judge of what it will study. In time, we shall hope that everything in reason—anything that is not positively hurtful—will be, so to say, "on tap," that is, available for study with positive help and encouragement. Naturally, we must begin with

what seems most insistent.   It is a great task we are undertaking and a long time will be required to get it all going.

And how will the study or work go on?   In every conceivable way, depending on what is being studied.   The
most common may be a small discussion-study group.   It
may be, however, a machine shop in which vocational
re-education is going on.   It may be a class working at
wood-carving under the guidance of some expert.   It
may be chorus singing under a leader.   It may be group
working with boys and girls in the cellar clubs of the
poorer districts.   It may be a class in English for for-
eigners.   It may be a group of foreign-born wives and
mothers learning better how to care for their children
and families under American conditions.   It may be a
group of lawyers and business men studying our money
system.

Whatever we do, we must get as far as possible away
from the teacher-assignment, pupil-recitation notion of
study.   To continue that would be just plain movement-
suicide.   Grown people will never stand for it, and should
not.   It is bad for children, too, if the truth be told.

Will the system be propagandist?   Where the matter
is controversial, no.   But where there is reasonable agreement among the capable in the field, genuine efforts will
be made to spread better practices, as we have long done
with agriculture and home-making.   Where the matter
is still controversial, care will be taken to have all significant options studied.   The system as a system must be
very careful not to be propagandist of any partisan position, particularly of the theory of the party that happens
then to be in power.   Contrariwise, the system must be

careful to foster the genuine study of any significant problem. The words *genuine study* give the proper answer to our question.

But are the lecturers not to be permitted to say what they honestly believe? Most certainly they will be so permitted; but they must know that it is study and not indoctrination that they are seeking. In particular, the system must afford in any public forum fair opportunity for the proponents of the unpopular side. This is the acid test of free speech and free study. We seek genuine study by the people.

When is all this to begin? It has already begun. The depression has helped to give it a great start. And we shall never permanently give up any part of it which shows that it serves a real need. This is the next great educational movement. It has begun. It will continue. May it come in fullness and speedily!

Part II

LIFE AND LEARNING

VIII
LIVING AND LEARNING*

IF I were a minister preaching a sermon, I should take as my text a quotation from a brilliant Britisher, W. K. Clifford, who died prematurely a half century ago. "It is," he said, "the peculiarity of living things not merely that they change under the influence of surrounding circumstances, but that any change . . . in them is not lost, but retained, and, as it were, built into the organism to serve as a foundation of future actions."† This quotation will perhaps serve to orient our thinking.

First of all, I ask you to consider with me the place of learning in active experience—life's learning; and in this I should like to contrast life's learning with school learning in the older conventional sense. Consider how, in any instance of active experience, learning goes on all the time. You probably have not thought about it so, but it is none the less true. In any instance of active experience, learning is going on at every moment of the experience; and, moreover, the learning is absolutely

---

* An address delivered in San Francisco in 1938.
† *Lectures and Essays*, London, 1891, p. 88.

necessary if what is then and there going on is to make
sense with itself.   We do not principally learn with reference to the future.   We principally learn with reference to that which is immediately at hand.   For instance,
in conversation, if you are talking with a person, you must
learn what he says right then and there; otherwise you
cannot reply intelligently to him.   Nay more, if you do
not learn the first half of any sentence, you cannot join
the second half with the first half to make sense.   You
see that learning is absolutely necessary to successful
listening, as successful listening is absolutely necessary
to appropriate rejoinder.   Also, when you engage in any
ordinary affair of life, such as buying a coat, if you did
not learn as you go, you would never lay aside this coat
and consider the next one as preferable.   You learn as you
go; if you did not learn the price of one in comparison
with another to act upon that price, you could not act intelligently.   In so simple a matter as buying a coat learning, therefore, is absolutely necessary in order that the
next stage of what you do may be built appropriately upon
what has just preceded.   So also in cooking a meal, and
so in eating it.   If you don't know whether you have put
salt on what you have just eaten; if you don't remember
whether the food suited you; if you do not so learn, you
cannot act intelligently about putting salt on it.   You
would be forever having it taste wrong but do nothing
about it if you did not learn as you lived.

However, it is more than memorizing that is involved.
Feelings are evoked and accepted to act upon.   Impulses
are evoked and, after more or less consideration, are accepted in some sense to act upon.   In fact, as you do

anything, there come forward thinking, feeling, and impulses evoked out of the experience; and for these to
serve in any experience they must be learned at this stage
of the experience in some sense in order that, by using
them as a foundation, you may intelligently go on to
the next stage. During any experience, at each moment
thoughts come forward to you as to what to do, how to
size up what has just been said, what to think about it.
Feelings, conceptions, and impulses arise in connection
with it, and you have to weigh these more or less and
accept them; and, if you accept them to act on, then they
are so built into your being that, using them as a foundation, you can go on to the next stage where other thoughts,
feelings, and impulses in turn arise; and these in turn
you weigh and accept in some sense and so go on to the
next forever. This is the actual process of experiencing.

In times past we have talked about learning as if it
went on rarely, as if it took place with difficulty, and as
if it necessarily required repetition. I am prepared to
defend the thesis that by all odds most of the learning
that goes on takes place at the moment the thing happens
and not by repetition. We hear or see what is done.
We size it up. We accept or reject it. And what we thus
accept to act upon is built at once, right then and there,
into character. Such learning involves no repetition except the further use of it in other experiences that will
give it additional connections, but usually there is no
repetition in order to get it learned.

I ask you, then, to note these several things. First, this
kind of life's learning is going on all the time when we
are awake and engaged about anything. It is going on

automatically. It is an inherent part of life's activity and hardly at all do we make any effort in such learning. The learning part of it comes of itself. We note what significance the situation has for us, the significance it has to our concerns, and we note this significance in the degree that we feel the situation. We learn anything in the degree that we grant significance to it. If it is of little significance, we learn it but slightly and soon forget it. If it is of great significance, we learn it deeply. It becomes grounded firmly into our being and we do not forget it. If you leave learning out of experience, experience would then have no logical consistency, no logical coherence. It is the learning that joins experience together to make it a continuing whole. Note also that what is so learned is built into the very structure of one's being, and so built in right then and there that we come out of the experience different because of what we have experienced; and the difference is exactly what we have learned. This becomes then the definition of learning. It is the change in one's makeup, the change in one's very being, brought about through one's actual experiencing. Clifford is justified. The facts substantiate his statement.

Now I am going to repeat this in part, this time using the term "response." To live is to act, and to act is to respond. We learn then our responses and nothing but them. When I hear you speak, I do not learn what you say. I learn what I think you said. I learn my response. I may not even learn what I think you said. I may learn what I think you mean, which may sometimes be somewhat different. We learn our responses exactly and—this may surprise you—we learn all of them, every one of them, in some sense and degree. As the response comes forward we weigh it, to accept it or not; and, if we accept it, then we learn it as we accept it. If we say no, that is not so, it is a mistake, then we learn it as we do accept it. We learn it with the reservations with which we accept it.

I may then sum up life's learning process to this stage of our discussion by using these words: We learn our responses, only our responses, and all of our responses. We learn them in the sense or in the direction in which we accept them to act upon (including under "acceptance" the negative kind of acceptance that we ordinarily call rejection). That is to say, we respond and then weigh that response and accept it as we count that it will fit into life, to be acted upon either positively or negatively. Also— I am summing up and so repeating—we learn our responses unequally: some as of more importance and others as of less importance.

We learn, then, our responses unequally, some as of more importance and others as of less, and the learning abides with us in the degree to which we count the matter significant. If it is of little significance, it abides but a little while. If it is of greater significance, it abides for a long time. What I have just said seems to be the basis of Thorndike's Law of Effect, that we learn to do what satisfies and learn not to do what annoys. It is also the basis of that older and less accurate statement that we learn to do what gives us pleasure and learn not to do what gives us pain. My way of saying it, that we learn it according to the way we accept it and in the degree that we accept it, takes both of those into account and, I think, corrects them.

Now, it appears to be true that practice or repetition may train a weak learning. We may not attach much significance to a thing the first time we hear it. Then we do not learn it very much. The next time we learn it, we learn it a little more, and the next time a little more. If that happens frequently enough, in the end we learn it strongly. This seems to be the way we learn things like telephone numbers, for instance. Of course, you may wish to learn your friend's telephone number and that wish makes it more significant for you and you therefore learn it more quickly, but a telephone number is not easy to learn because there are so few thought connections. However, if somebody tells you that a person lives next door to your friend and you know perfectly well where your friend lives, you have no trouble remembering where this new person lives because you have a ready-made system to fit it into. But in ordinary instances, repetition seems to help, as we have always known.

Now, I should like to go through with this same discussion in a more formal fashion in order to bring out other elements not present in what has been said. Suppose we take any active experience. It may be buying a coat (as was suggested just above), or it may be a woman cooking a meal—and if she is not used to cooking, that is a very active experience. She has to think a great deal about it while she is doing it. At the beginning of any experience and at any new phase of the experience, first of all *we note and distinguish* things that are pertinent to our interests. We may notice other things, but we notice especially things pertinent to our interests.

Secondly, *we relate* what we note. We may relate part of what we note with another part of what we note, or we may relate what we note to other things previously learned, but we relate what we note with reference to what to do about it, with reference to following up our concern. Thirdly, *we accept* in some sense and degree what we have related and accept it *in some way to act upon it.*

This acceptance, as was said earlier, includes rejection as a possible negative instance. It also includes the varying conditions under which we accept. For instance, a mother might say to her son, "Stop pulling the cat's tail." Now, what does the child do? He pays attention to the tone of voice his mother uses. If she speaks as if she "means business," then he relates tone with words and accepts that he had better not pull the cat's tail, at any rate right away, and he learns it that way and acts accordingly. If he is very anxious to pull the cat's tail, he may say to himself: "It won't do for her to find me pulling the cat's tail," so that he may accept it as not to pull the cat's tail where she will find it out. Many people learn to accept things this way. Or, this boy may be extraordinary and learn that he is not to pull the cat's tail at all at any time. If he learns it that way, he acts accordingly. But he learns it as he accepts it, according to the conditions put upon it when he accepts it. That is the way our children learn when we talk to them in school. They learn it with the conditions which they accept with it, and they build it into character that way. To sum up, *we note and distinguish* with reference to our interests, *we relate* with reference to the pursuit of those interests and *we accept* in some sense *to act upon;* and then, fourth, *what we accept we build into character,* into organic structure. We build it into our very own being then and there according to the way we accept it, with the limitations with which we accept it and to the degree we accept it. And character is thus built. It is being built all of the time. During every instant of life this child is noting and relating and accepting to act upon in some sense, and he is building what he accepts into his character.

This process, I say, is going on all of the time, and the new that is thus accepted is interwoven with the old. The new remakes the old and the old remakes the new, and this interpenetration of old with new and new with old is what makes character. Character is not a mere aggregate of habits. Character is the interpenetration of old and new so that a new-old comes out, is continually coming out. Children, then, are building character all the time. I frequently read in some books, in some courses of study, in some discussions of curriculum, about "character education." This taken by itself is a very inadequate conception. Character building goes on all the time. You can't take it out and give it a special period, 10 to 10:20 each day. You can have a special period if you wish, but character building won't restrict itself to that period.

I should now like to sum up the whole discussion again, using this time the verb "to live." Consider this meaning of the verb: "Our children will not really learn democracy unless they *live* democracy." And again, "It is better always to *live* poetry than to write poetry." Let us take that sense of the verb "to live" and in terms of it restate what I have been talking about as follows: We learn what we live. We learn what we really at bottom live, what we mean as we live. We learn what we live in the degree that we live it, in the degree and within the limitations with which we accept it to act upon. We shall not learn anything unless we live it. And what we thus learn we build therein at once into organic structure.

These things have serious consequences for us who are parents or for us who are teachers. If children learn what they live, if they learn and so build into character what they live, then the quality of that living is the most important thing that can happen in the life of that child. Let me repeat: If children learn what they live, the quality of their living is what counts. If this child lives a high quality of life, he builds a high quality of character. If he lives a low quality of life and accepts that as his way of living, then he builds that quality of living into his character. Our children will learn what they live at bottom, what they live in their hearts and so choose as their way of living. That is after all what counts. As a man purposeth in his heart so is he and so he becomes.

If these things are true, the most important thing of all while these children are in school, or at home, or on the playground or anywhere—the most important thing is the *quality* of the living. And if it is what they feel in their hearts that counts, what can we do? How can we make them feel what we would wish them to feel in their hearts? Our part is at best indirect. We cannot control their hearts. The quality of living is like the quality of mercy: it cannot be constrained; it wells up from within. "Out of the heart are the issues of life." Though our part is indirect at best, still we can help. We can help partly by giving opportunity to the good and finer things, partly by stimulation, and partly by encouragement when the finer and better things come. And, less surely, we can help negatively by refusing to allow bad things to be done outwardly. But refusal is dangerous because it is what goes on in the heart that counts, and refusal on our part often brings strong negative reaction within.

The chief thing for us, then, is that we understand these things, that we understand that the subject matter which we have been too much teaching in our schools may be the least significant thing in life. How often is it true that these children do not live the history or the geography, that they do not accept it in any inward sense, do not relate it in any true sense to life? If so, it is barely learned. The word "learned" hardly fits. The learnings that go along by the side of this sort of learning, the concomitant learnings, the attitudes that are being built—these may be far more important than the subject matter we think we are teaching. This child may be learning arithmetic. We say that is what he is learning. He is doing far more. He is building the attitude of liking this arithmetic or not. He is building the attitude that he will, or will not, let it alone as soon as he can get rid of us. He may be building the attitude that he does not like us or anything connected with school. Children are in danger of building such attitudes, and these attitudes count for more and continue longer in life than the subject matter we teach. We must keep forever before us that the child does learn what he lives and does build his heart's acceptance into character. What at the bottom of his heart he accepts for himself, that he builds into character; and it is that which counts in life.

We must, then, as it seems to me, get a new and different concern about the process of education. Our concern should be not that the child shall learn the subject matter so that he can stand examination upon it. That may touch his life only superficially. Our real concern should be how to induce and encourage living—living of the finer and higher quality, living of such quality that we are willing to have it built into character. And probably the chief test of our success with the lives of our children is as to how far we have helped these children build such a life that from within it wells up ever new life, ever finer life. We know the difference when we see it. We know that sometimes children are alive, awake, eager. We know that at other times just the opposite is true. This, then, becomes our chief test and our chief aim for our children, that they shall really live. For they will learn what they live, what they in their innermost souls choose as their way of living.

If these things are so, then we have to consider more seriously, more fundamentally than we have been willing to do, the kind of work that should go on in our schools. I do not know how you feel about it, but when I think that our children will learn what they live, will learn the very quality of the lives they are living, it seems the most serious thought that I know and our responsibility becomes very great. We must somehow help them to live lives worthy of being built into character.

IX
HOW LEARNING TAKES PLACE

THE aim here is to help to more adequate dealing with people. The effort will be to discuss the learning process in such way that educators in general, teachers, and leaders of groups in particular, may better see how to deal with youth for their best growth in and for life in a democratic society. What is here presented is in part new, and in part old. Perhaps its chief characteristic is the insistence it makes that learning be conceived as an essential part of the experience process itself, of every experience as it now goes on. How this is true and what difference it makes for teachers and leaders will, it is hoped, become clearer as the discussion proceeds.

The Life Process

Life is the continual interaction between an organism and its environment. Something happens either within or without the organism, or *between* the organism and its environment, which stirs the organism to action. Whether that action be to seek or to avoid, either is goal-seeking. The organism thus responds to the situation it confronts and (as we shall in a moment consider) it responds as a whole. Looked at "within," as we frequently say, this response shows itself as want, wish, preference, inner urge, striving. Looked at without, we see

movements of body and limb, co-ordinated movements
of eye and ear and body and foot.

These movements are (typically) not random nor hap-
hazard, but are related to the particular want or urge
then felt. The movements in fact tend in the aggregate
to get what the organism wants: for example, to find
something to eat, or to avoid this enemy. At first these
movements may fail. If so, they (typically) vary, either
to become more vigorous or to change in direction or
kind, and they continue as a rule until either the want
is met or failure is established.

Such movements as those just described we call efforts.
The animal is "making efforts" to find food, or is "making
efforts" to ward off his enemy. His behavior is true goal-
seeking. Man also makes efforts, and his efforts may
differ from those of the lower animal in being conscious
and intentional in a degree and in a sense, so it appears,
not true of any other animal.

Ends in Behavior

Certain important terms emerge together from this
discussion, terms that much concern us, such as efforts,
aim, end, purpose, means, goal-seeking, success, failure,
conscious, intentional, purposive, purposeful. Some of
these, such as aim, purpose, intentional, purposeful, belong (we believe) peculiarly to man. The others man
shares with many of the higher animals. Such terms are
called telic or teleological because they refer to ends or
aims. Some psychologists, who like, mistakenly, to think
of themselves as more scientific than others, fight shy of

all such terms and the conceptions that underlie them. They try to explain behavior mechanistically, and accordingly shun all use of ends and means. But to discuss life and behavior without reference to wants and efforts is to leave out of the behavior of all higher animals its most distinctive feature, just as it is to miss the most distinctly human element if we try to get on without reference to purposes and the conscious choice of means. The effort is as unnecessary and unscientific as it is futile.

To sum up and apply this thesis, we may well conceive a scale of different kinds of behavior, the most consciously directed at the "high" end, and the least so at the "low." Learning, which is our fundamental quest here, will be found to differ for different parts of this scale. Man is capable of learning at all points of the scale, but it is the learning that goes on in the upper half that most concerns us here; for in it is the human aspect of man most clearly and distinctively at work.

The Organism Acting as a Whole

It was intimated above that, in behaving, the organism acts "as a whole." A word of explanation as to the meaning of this phrase may not be amiss. The simplest explanation is to take the word organism as meaning what it says. The organism, since it is an organism, acts like an organism. That is, the organism is some sort of an organization, an organized unity, and so acts. Who has not seen through a window a cat clearly intent on some object not in sight to the observer? It is easy to tell whether the cat is getting ready to pounce on some small object, say, a bird or chipmunk, which it looks forward to

catching and eating; or whether the cat is preparing to
fight off a bigger animal that it fears, say, a dog. These
two "sets" of the cat are clearly distinct; no one could
mistake which one is operating. And "the whole" cat
is most surely involved and organized for appropriate
action—eyes, nerves, muscles, body, limbs, all are
acting co-operatively to further the effort the cat is making. And the most careful studies of Sherrington and
others corroborate what here appears evident. There are
degrees of set and readiness, but the whole organism acts,
typically if not always, as one whole, part co-operating
with part to further the effort the organism is making.
Whether in man or beast, the organism acts as a whole.

Selfhood

In any full discussion of human conduct the conception
of selfhood is essential. Through what he learns from in-
teracting with his environment man builds up meanings;
he makes, as has been discussed, his own organization of
meanings. Through the use of the cultural accumulation and language as partially embodying it, the human
infant comes to see himself as one in the company of
other persons, understanding himself in terms of what he
sees in them, understanding them in terms of what
(largely through the use of language) he now sees in himself. In this way he can look, now to the past and now
to the future, and understand more or less of how they
are related. He can think of himself as effecting this or
that, and, accordingly, as responsible for the results of
what he does. In these ways he can plan and hold himself to account for probable consequences. In other

words, in and through selfhood and the means through which it is achieved, the growing child builds the more adequate use of language, acquires usable knowledge, purposes, plans, executes, judges, accepts moral responsibility—in a word, grows into the fullness of life that we see actual in the better adults.

Set and Readiness

Reference was made above to the cat and her "set" to catch the bird or her "set" to ward off the dog. A few words further on this will perhaps prove helpful in the future discussion. It seems clear that, corresponding to each characteristic upset, or stirring to action, on the part of the cat there is an appropriate "set"; and this is in fact a set to action—action appropriate to the want thus stirred. The term "readiness" is often used in this connection, and some find difficulty in distinguishing "set" from "readiness." It seems better to think of the "set" as abiding throughout the whole episode, from beginning to end, and as including the whole organism. Readiness, on the other hand, is thought of as more precisely located in those parts of the organism likely to be called next into play by the developing episode and therefore as shifting from part to part as the drama unfolds in time. The cat is set on the chipmunk as an object of prey throughout the whole episode, but at one stage its muscles and nerves for stalking are the ones to act next, then those having to do with pouncing, then (if the pouncing fails and the chipmunk is about to get away) those having to do with running, then catching, and finally devouring. As the drama unfolds, varying behavior is successively called forth, and just before the actual movements take place at any stage there is readiness, a keying up for better action, in the nerves and muscles likely to be called into play in that stage.

Humans also experience set and readiness. Purpose is a set for which a defined end has been set up after more or less of conscious choice. Purpose then belongs better, if not only, to man. Purposes differ in strength and in degree of internal unity (whole-heartedness), and readinesses in result differ accordingly. Also, the stronger the purpose, the greater the hindrance one can face without giving up. This last fact prepares the way for understanding unreadiness. When one is set on a certain purpose or end, he is (as an observable fact) psychologically ready to consider and deal with anything that seems to further that end, and (on the whole) correspondingly unready to consider anything that would divert him from that end. In this way, set, readiness, and unreadiness are psychological preparations for more efficient action, for the more efficient pursuit of the object defined by the set or purpose. The three together mean concentration upon the task of pursuing the end in view.

In connection with the conscious pursuit of purposes, readiness serves in two highly significant ways. One is that, in so far as we are set upon any end in view, in like degree are thoughts pertinent to that end likely to come to mind. This as an observed fact will vary enormously, depending partly on what one knows in the area concerned, and partly on how well one has his pertinent knowledge organized for use along the lines needed. This principle we shall find very important when we come to consider purposeful behavior and learning. The second application is related: namely, that the more fully one is set upon any end in view (short of painful solicitude) the more likely is he to have creative thoughts in that connection. This again will vary even more than the preceding, depending partly on the creative ability of the person engaged, partly on the range and organization of one's knowledge in the field. How set and readiness thus make more available what resources one has, proves highly significant for life and learning.

Interest

So far we have used the terms set, readiness, and purpose. A further frequent term is interest, which again is often misunderstood. The term is used in two senses, the one as a more abiding attitude that one carries around with him—many, many of them at the same time—waiting suitable stimulation to be stirred into overt activity. This may be called the structural sense of interest. Each such is the abiding possibility of set and readiness, of purpose, of attention, concern, and action along its line. The second sense becomes apparent when the structural interest is in fact active. Set and readiness along that line are now at work. Thus, one may have many interests: tennis, grand opera, deep-sea fishing, a rock garden, astronomy, teaching, Smithfield ham. As a rule, only one of these will be active at any one time. When any one is so active, it brings set and readiness and unreadiness appropriately in its train to determine attention and effort. In the degree one is unified within on any course of action, in the degree that he is, inwardly, interested in that course of action, he, outwardly, puts forth efforts to pursue it. Interest and effort are thus not only not opposed to each other; they are but two names for one unified ongoing activity, which we call interest when we look within and effort when we look without.

Life and the Organic Conserving of Experience

The preceding chapter referred to a quotation from W. K. Clifford, which will be repeated here and discussed somewhat: "It is the peculiarity of living things not merely that they change [that is, behave] under the influence of surrounding circumstances, but that any change [behavior] which takes place in them is not lost, but retained, and, as it were, built into the organism to serve as a foundation for future actions."

This is a fundamental statement. If we contrast, as Clifford proceeds to do, the inorganic with the organic, the difference between the two appears precisely in the words quoted. Gold, for example, may be molded into a ring and then melted down and re-molded into, say, a pin. If so, the gold in the second state carries no perceptible trace of its earlier "experience." Molding into the pin went on as if the gold had never been molded into a ring. But with the living thing, each experience it goes through somehow changes it so that it behaves differently thereafter. Life accumulates itself in and through the living, so that prior experience remains to influence the present and future.

What has just been said holds of the lower animals, but it holds, for our purposes, more interestingly of man. Take any developing experience, such as happens to all of us every day: A man calls me on the telephone to tell me that things are going badly in a matter that concerns us both. As I take in the situation, what I "take in" begins at once to shape not only the rest of that conversation, but helps determine for some days to come—and long thereafter—both how I shall feel and what I shall do in respect to the matter of concern. A man we had trusted had played us false; it became necessary to take legal steps to protect our interests; only after many and laborious efforts were things once more set straight. I am changed from thenceforth—I meet that man as a somewhat different person because of the transaction, the incident enters into my further dealings in the enterprise, my other concerns in so far as they were affected must take account of this.

Here is life actually going on as life does for good or ill with all people: the housewife with the butcher, with her husband, with the children; the man with his family, with his business enterprises, with his friends; the teacher or group leader with the members of his group, with his superior officers, with his fellow workers. The significant thing here is that conscious life is cumulative, and each successive phase of the experience is affected not only by what has gone before but it in turn enters as a factor into what follows to help determine the character of the rest of the experience.

And note that the organism acts as a whole throughout such an experience. I not only talked, I thought, I felt, I decided, I experienced impulses, I made purposes. All parts and aspects of my being were involved, and these various parts or phases of experience were included in the cumulative effects of the experience.

And note again, my attention was selective and the cumulative effects were the results of my selective attention. In this attention, certain of my stock of abiding interests were deciding factors. The enterprise mentioned above is one of my interests. When the phone call came, that particular interest was dormant, and it stayed so until the pertinence of the threat began to dawn. Then that interest became active. Appropriate set and readinesses followed. I asked questions that welled up creatively within, called up as readinesses by the set (the interest in the enterprise as aroused by the threat). Thus does life go on. Clifford is right. I not only responded under the influence of these circumstances, but these responses of mine were not lost; they were retained, built as it were at once into the structure of my being, there to serve as foundation for the next successive phases of the experience and also, as may be needed, in further and later experiences.

This analysis and illustration of the Clifford thesis is the point and essence of all that follows. The life process is like this. In such an analysis of the life process the fact of learning gets its best definition.

Learning

To get a clear definition of learning, let us first look back over the analysis of this telephone experience to distinguish process and structure. William James speaks of the stream of consciousness. We could also call it the stream of experience. As we look at life going on, at the stream of experience, we can distinguish the content of what is going on at any moment as the process—the life process—and we can see in this some elements or factors that have come over from the past. Let us fix attention, for the moment, on these elements or factors that come over from what has gone before. These we shall call structure. When the telephone rang, it was a present occurrence, a present experience. Life was in process. It was, however, not simply a noise that I heard; it was a telephone call. In the past I had met and identified the peculiar ring of the telephone as contrasted with the doorbell or other noises; I recognized it now for what it was. Saved over from the past as structure was the basis of my recognition. Similarly, I had brought over the habit and skill of using a telephone. These two were structure that helped determine process in the next phase of the experience. So also when I heard the name of the one speaking to me, I had as already existing structure these general things: my knowledge of the man's name, my knowledge of the man that belonged with the name, my opinion of him and of his character, and my various reaction-tendencies connected with these several structure elements. I had known him well and considered him the kind of man whose word and integrity I could not question. All these things entered as structure while and as I heard and took in the threat to my interests. Had a man of different standing spoken, I might have doubted what I was told. If so, I should have acted differently. This doubt, itself true structure, would have entered the subsequent experience to help determine the further process of my thinking and acting.

So we have the contrasted but related terms, structure and process. The process is not simply the fact and presence of structure; it is rather the functioning of structure. And even more: New things enter into the process, some from the situation, some from me. On both new counts, and otherwise, this particular process never happened before. True enough, many preceding experiences will show similarities. Many times has the telephone called me, with people speaking at the other end; but never before these precise words spoken, and never have come just these reactions from me. It seems correct (at least measurably so) to say that the structure can be used over and over again, but that the resulting process is always unique.

Using these terms, structure and process, we can now define the term *to learn* as our name for the fact that life somehow builds process into structure—into structure that is thenceforth ready to be called into play to help determine subsequent processes. Learning then is the crucial factor at work in Clifford's thesis that any change [behavior] which takes place in the living thing is not lost, but is built into the structure of the organism, there to serve as the foundation of further action.

Learning is thus going on at least during all the time that one is awake and alert. Moreover, it is this fact of learning that makes it possible for the earlier phases of an experience to affect the later. Nay more, it is the fact of learning that makes experience out of what would otherwise be mere successive atomistic happenings. Through the fact of learning, each successive earlier phase and stage of an experience remains in existence to enter into and color all the rest. It is solely through learning that the cumulative effect in experience is made possible. In a word, it is the fact of continual learning that gives logical coherence to any instance of experience.

Therefore, instead of being a laborious affair (as many in and out of school still think) to be effected mainly by irksome repetition and usable only in some more or less remote future, learning is mainly an automatic and instantaneous affair, springing naturally out of the life process, with repetition before practical use the exception rather than the rule. Moreover, nearly all learning is put to use at once within the very experience in which it takes place. In fact (so it appears), it is for this primary service that learning comes into existence; and without such learning, life as we know it and value it would not go on. Continuous learning is necessary to conscious existence and pertinent action.

Acceptance an Essential Factor in Learning

It was implicit in the whole preceding discussion on learning that the process was somehow built into structure. We should remind ourselves at this point of the discussion in the preceding chapter: what is built into structure is our own responses, and only our own responses. In the telephone conversation any mis-hearings or misunderstandings or misinterpretations that were part of my responses were built into structure accordingly. I learn the meanings that I have myself constructed as best I can out of the sounds that reach my ear. The same thing holds for seeing, for feeling, for understanding. The more we think about it, the clearer it becomes that I learn not *the* facts, the absolute facts (if there are such), but the facts as I see them, as I get them and report them to myself. I learn my responses precisely as I accept them to act on, my responses positively and my responses negatively, what I accept and what I reject.

With this understanding we can now state our first and most inclusive principle of learning, as follows:

Principle A: We learn our responses, only our responses, all our responses, and we learn each as we accept it to act on.

Degrees of Acceptance on a Scale

It was pointed out earlier that we can distribute behavior on a scale according to the degree of conscious and deliberate thought that enters into it. In the same way, we can distribute the fact of acceptance according to the degree of conscious deliberation that enters into the accepting. Thus, in the classic experiments, Pavlov's dog, which was conditioned to secrete saliva at the sound of a bell, learned so to behave because he accepted (on his level of acceptance) the sound of the bell as the sign of the coming meat. We see that this is true because, if the meat was not forthcoming often enough to maintain the expectation, the dog ceased so to react, and the conditioning lapsed. The same principle of acceptance we may believe holds also of trial-and-error learning, though this seems to belong still lower in the scale.

Forgetting; Varying Strength of Learning

That we forget; that we remember some things better than others; that some skills lessen if not kept alive by appropriate practice—these are facts known by all men. Put together, they lead to the conception of strength of learning. Some learnings, or some instances of learning, seem to stick better, or last longer than others. It is clearly to the advantage of a person to be master of what he has learned, whether of knowledge or skill, in order that he may call it up at will for use.

The question then arises as to the conditions favorable to strength of learning. If we know these conditions, we may be able to use them to our advantage. Many observations and experiments have been made by psychologists on this question, but unfortunately they differ among themselves as to the proper answers. The following statements of principle seem to this writer at once the best supported and the most serviceable.

Principle B: We learn anything in the degree that we count it significant.

By significant is here meant, of course, significant to the learner, having what seems an important bearing on what he values. If my house burns down, it will be more significant to me (other things being equal), than if my friend's house burns, and still more significant than if it were a stranger's house that burned. I shall therefore learn my own house burning more strongly than my friend's, and still more strongly than the stranger's.

This principle can be restated in terms of strength of response—a form that at times will prove more useful. If I count a matter significant, I shall respond more strongly. And also, so it appears, if I respond more strongly, I shall count the matter more significant. Which of these two ways of looking at the matter is more fundamental may be debated, but it seems fairly sure that the stronger the response, other things being equal, the stronger the learning. We may then restate Principle B as follows:

Principle B': We learn in the degree that we respond.

This wording joins the principle more closely with the wording of Principle A.

This Principle B' is meant to be only an alternative form to Principle B. But there is more that can be said: When my own house burns, not only do I feel it more strongly, but I also think more about it than I should about my friend's house or about a stranger's house. My house, especially if the contents were burnt with it, is connected in many ways with various parts and aspects of my life. From time to time for months and even for years I am reminded of things destroyed in the fire, many never to be replaced. Such an experience not only cuts deep, but it cuts at many points. I learn it very deeply and with many interrelationships. These considerations of the many connections suggest another principle:

Principle C: We learn anything in the degree that it is connected in many ways with things already well known.

Many practical applications follow from Principle C. For one thing, the more we think over what we do and the more we can relate particular matters to general principles, the more surely can we expect to hold them available for recall. It follows that a conscious scheme, logically organized, is a great help. But if it is to help me, it must be my scheme; mine, that is, in the sense that I have made it to be my own even if I first got the idea from somewhere else. Merely to memorize items that had been arranged according to somebody else's system probably will not make the learning systematic for me. I must think the system myself. To see things as fundamentally related, for example, by causation, is especially good. In one final word, it is the multiplicity of conscious and meaningful relationships that furnishes the key to the wise use of Principle C.

Repetition and Learning

It was formerly thought that repetition was the royal road to effective learning, and the idea is not yet dead. In fact, the idea ought not to die entirely. The essential facts relating to the problem are a bit complex, but not difficult, it seems, to understand.

In the first place, bare repetition, repetition that is meaningless to the learner, is next to impossible as a way of learning. Repetition alone brings no learning.*

Also, an over-reliance on repetition may do specific harm. Drill is frequently uninteresting and may be boring. According to Principle B we learn our responses as we accept them. If so, and the drill is boring enough, our pupils may learn to dislike the subject boringly or unsuccessfully drilled upon, dislike the teacher who directs the drill, dislike the school, and even dislike the whole business of books. Our pupils will learn the way they feel about what they do. These considerations thoroughly condemn the old steady diet of drill and memorization.

There is, however, a real place for practice, for repeat-

---

* See Thorndike, E. L., *Human Learning*. New York, D. Appleton-Century Co., 1931. Lecture I.

ing the learning experience. Any ordinary learning experience seldom yields, by the one experience, learning of the strongest possible degree. For this reason, repeating the learning experience under varying conditions at not too long intervals is frequently necessary to make one master of the new idea or fact or skill. But it must not be forgotten that the amount of repetition necessary to give mastery will, as a rule, vary inversely with the felt significance of the matter: the more meaningful the work, the less drill is necessary. We may then conclude, as a first approximation, that the more drill we find going on, the poorer the learning situation.

Before leaving the subject, we should point out that practice is not necessarily the same thing as drill or mere repetition. Suppose one is learning a golf stroke. At first, he will do it badly. Mere repetition of this bad stroke is not what is needed, but a kind of practice that varies the stroke, in order that progress may be made, largely by trial and error, to a more desirable form. This practice is, emphatically, not mere repetition.

Purpose and Learning

Although much more might be said about the place of purpose in learning, fortunately the main discussion has already been given (on pp. 81-84) when we studied purpose, set, readiness and unreadiness. That purpose, in the degree to which it is present, means efficiency of action was perhaps there sufficiently brought out. What concerns us now is how purpose helps learning. The discussion divides itself into two main heads: (1) how one's purpose helps in learning the things needed for carrying out the purpose; (2) how one's purpose affects the building of attitudes and generalizations that accompany the carrying out of the purpose.

1. As regards learning what is needed to carry out the purpose. In all learning there is (a) a proposing of what to think, or how to feel, or what to do—possibly several choices of proposals; and (b) there is an acceptance of a choice as to what thought or feeling or plan to act on. Favorable learning conditions show themselves under both heads: conditions favorable to good (useful, appropriate) proposals and conditions favorable to hearty acceptance.

That purpose brings better proposals has already been seen in the discussion above referred to on purpose, set, and readiness. Purpose as a set brings a higher degree of readiness both for the recall of what one knows and can do, and for creative thinking. Either by itself would mean better proposals than otherwise would obtain, while both together promise still better proposals. And these statements hold whether one has or has not sufficient resources already present within himself. If he has to go outside himself for help, to other persons or to books, his purpose and set still hold to make him wish to do these things if they be necessary and to make mind and ear or eye ready as he talks or reads. In all this, it is also true that the aim or end of the purpose gives the needed basis for selective attention and discriminating thinking and later on furnishes as well the basis for testing what has been thought and done. From these various considerations, it stands clear that the stronger the purpose (short of too painful solicitude), the better the pro-

posals that one will make available to himself for dealing
with the situation.

It is equally clear that purpose brings clear-cut and
stronger acceptance and therefore stronger learning.
Purpose, in the degree that it is present, means a well-
defined end and aim. We know what we want, and we
are therefore the better prepared to judge any relevant
proposals; being better prepared to judge, we are therefore better prepared to accept definitely and strongly,
or to reject definitely and strongly, whatever does or does
not meet our needs. But definite and strong acceptance
(or rejection) means strong learning. The stronger the
purpose, the stronger the learning.

2. As regards learning attitudes and generalizations,
we never learn just one thing; always are we also learning
how we think and feel about what is happening.

As to attitudes, we learn all our responses, including
specifically how we feel about our work and about anything connected with it. If in the end we like what we
work with, our successive acceptances of liking will build
favorable attitudes toward that thing, probably toward
the teacher who works with it, probably toward the school
in which such things go on, and in particular toward the
subject or area in which this work lies. If, on the contrary, we are not interested in what we are doing and wish
to be working with something else, then we shall probably respond with dislike to our work, and if these dislikes are sufficiently repeated, we shall build an abiding
attitude of dislike, or perhaps even of hatred, of what
we have been doing and of the things especially connected with it. Although the presence of purpose does

not guarantee good results here, it still makes more probable an initial interest in what one is doing, with therefore stronger efforts, and besides brings with it a personal
commitment. The stronger the purpose, then, the
stronger will one stand by it, and the greater will be the
likelihood of success. From these various considerations,
the stronger the purpose, the greater the probability that
favorable attitudes will be built.

As to generalizations, the discussion is different. Each
one always generalizes more or less; and the more one
thinks about a thing with a wish to be master of it, the
more and better generalizations are probable. So again,
the stronger the purpose the greater the probability that
one will think constructively about the matter and therefore the more likely will helpful generalization follow.
And this also holds whether one has or has not in himself
sufficient resources for thinking out the useful generalization. Teachers are, if anything, more necessary here
than elsewhere. But if so, the stronger the purpose, the
more favorably disposed will the pupils be for aid coming
from the teacher's interest and help in the matter.

In all these matters, it thus appears true that the
stronger the pupil's purpose, the greater the probability
of strong and healthy learnings.

Coercion and Learning

Coercion is just the opposite of purpose, and has (in
nearly all respects) exactly the opposite effects on learning. In purpose, the motive to act is from within; in
coercion it is from without. The essence of coercion lies
in presenting a pupil with what is to him a choice of

evils: a lesser evil (what the teacher wishes done), and a greater evil (the punishment or other threat) such that the pupil will prefer the other (lesser) evil. Under such circumstances, the pupil will learn something because he does, in a degree (under the circumstances), wish to do the disagreeable thing at least well enough to avoid the punishment. But as against this wish, he has his initial set in the opposite direction. This set brings internal unreadiness. As a result, in general the favorable set and readiness that purpose supplies are here exactly reversed, at least after a certain minimum has been met: The pupil is unready to think much, unlikely to do creative thinking; he cares a little to succeed, but not much; and he will probably dislike what he is doing for the double reason that he was initially opposed to it, and he dislikes being made to do it. It is, of course, true, as at times in music lessons, that what began as coercion changes into interest as unexpected success develops. But this is the exception and is usually due to unsuspected gifts. On the whole, coercion is bad for learning: The instrumental learning is likely to be less strong; and of the attendant learnings, the attitudes are likely to be unfavorable and the generalizations less well made. Except as an emergency measure, to avoid a worse evil, the wise teacher will avoid coercion.

Conclusion

Of the discussion herein given on learning two things may in conclusion be said. First, that the presentation has been from an organismic point of view; goal-seeking has been stressed, not minimized. Secondly, the stress has been on the human rather than on the animal side and aspect of man. This is not to deny conditioning, or trial and error learning, or drill and rote memory; but it is to give these a place of subordinate importance.

The aim has been to find and present a psychology of learning useful for guiding youth within the American scene. Our young people, as they face life now and later, must learn, each for himself and all together, how to map out a fitting course of action and pursue it. No such self-direction will be adequate unless it first of all is able to find and face without evasion the pertinent facts of each confronting situation. This is to build the integrated personality. And further, an adequate self-direction must in its decisions take an ever broader range of possible results of action into effective account. Specifically, all selfish and merely personal interests must increasingly be subordinated to the common and impartial welfare of all concerned, oneself counting simply as one among the rest. To present a theory of learning that would help leaders best to effect these things has been the guiding aim throughout.

X

BASIC AIMS IN MODERN EDUCATION*

No EFFORT can be directed consciously or (as a rule) efficiently, except as the guiding end or aim be clear. If we do not know what we are aiming at, we are not likely to score many hits.

In education, as in all moral undertakings, the question of aim is complicated by the fact that there are always multiple results simultaneously following any efforts we put forth; and we who act are morally responsible for all these simultaneous results. Even if we who teach pick one result as our specific and conscious aim—it may be for this child to learn to write or this other child to learn to add fractions or for this class to understand the American Revolution or for these older pupils to decide they are to think about company unions—whatever result we pick out as aim, we cannot morally disregard the other possible results that simultaneously follow what we and our pupils do. For, let us be assured, in education always are many things being learned together, and we who teach are responsible, as far as taking thought can go, for all these varied learning results.

Thus, while this child is having trouble with adding his fractions, he is not only learning how to add fractions well or badly, but he is building besides attitudes toward

---

* *New York State Education,* October, 1939.

fractions: whether they are things for him to fear or not and therefore whether things to hate or not. Further, he is building attitudes toward himself, whether he is or is not a "dumbbell" in fractions and perhaps in all arithmetic, and perhaps in all school learning. And still further—and very, very important—whether it pays to try. And, in close connection, whether he is to look out upon life hopefully and actively or whether to accept inferiority as his rôle. Whether teachers, parents, and all others who govern, are for him or against him; whether governing is not simply a device in which the strong use their power to prey upon the weak.

We need not think that all children think just these things about everything they do. But such things as these do go on, more or less consciously, all the time, and day in and day out they do add up until personality gets relatively set, it may be for good, it may be for ill. And children feel secure, or they feel insecure, as they face parents and teachers; they feel that they can face life, or they fear to face life; they feel that law and order is for them or against them; they feel that books and learning are for them, or are not to have any real part in their lives.

If we apply such questions to the adolescents under our care, we have not only all these same personality problems, but we have the social outlooks that they are forming to take along with them, more or less definitely, throughout life. All children, just because they are children, form inadequate conceptions of the deeper matters of life: of right and wrong and what makes it so, of government, of democracy, of proper attitudes toward social differences; if they be the children of "labor," what to think about those who oppose labor unions; if they be the children of the better-to-do, what to think about unions, and strikes, and the unemployed; if children of the unemployed, what to think of the world they live in, and the future they face. We who teach adolescents have, therefore, the serious task of helping them revise these inadequate conceptions to something more adequate. Otherwise, democratic citizenship fails.

It is this fact of multiple results that always follow life, however lived, that makes education so serious a problem. It is this fact of multiple results, coupled with the further fact that we learn what we live—the feelings we accept to live by, the thoughts we accept to act upon, the decisions we accept to act out in life—these facts taken together mean that our children are all the time building their characters and so all the time spinning their fates. This goes on all the time, and we teachers are responsible in so far as we can, by taking thought, affect results.

The most important of all questions for the teacher thus becomes: What kind of lives are these children living? What is the quality of the lives that they are building thus into character? Are we as teachers doing the best possible by our pupils? Are we really concerned about the personalities and characters they are building? Or do we forget character and personality as we stress the subjects we think we have been appointed to teach, as we urge our pupils on to good records in examinations?

It is such fundamental considerations as the foregoing that help us to state the basic aims of education.

1. The inclusive aim of education cannot be split up

into a number of separate items, each of which is to be
sought (for the time being) by itself. The child is one.
He is learning all the ways in which he is reacting. While
he is learning what to think or how to do, he is at the
same time learning how to feel about, and how to judge,
each thing and each phase of each thing that he thinks
about. These things are going on all the time, and he
is learning it all, building it all into personality and life.
The inclusive aim thus takes in everything that is all
the while going on.

2. Any picking out of some results to aim at, in disregard of the rest, is immoral—immoral in the highest
degree. For the teacher to say, "I am hired to teach
physics or English or mathematics or Latin; I must get
my pupils promoted, or get them through their examinations; I cannot take on these additional questions of character and personality"—for the teacher to say such things
is to show moral incompetence. There can be no justification for such an attitude. It is wrong, fundamentally
wrong, and wrong forever.

3. As we consider the future lives of our pupils we can,
at least roughly, recognize that some learnings are more
important than others.

(1) Most important perhaps of all are the emotional
attitudes that make up the well-adjusted personality: the sense of inner security as one faces life,
an acceptable recognition among one's fellows, the
ability and disposition to face reality without evasion, absence of hurtful inferiority complexes and
the like. Such things lie at the base of all else.

No other learning got at the expense of these can
be justified.

(2) Physical health, which needs no discussion here.
Next after "mental" health, it is basic to all else.

(3) Ability to get on well with other people, to be
able and disposed to treat others courteously and
justly, able to share in discussion and come to conclusions, able and disposed to co-operate effectively in action.

(4) Appreciation and understanding of current social life so as to be able to take effective part in
running a democratic society.

(5) In general, the ability and disposition to act on
thinking.

4. Of lesser importance than the foregoing (that is,
these must not be got at the expense of the preceding),
are the following:

(1) Vocational preparation. This is highly important
not only for the money it brings, but perhaps even
more for its bearing on personality, which was
put first on the foregoing list. Fortunately, these
various ends are not mutually exclusive.

(2) Such learnings as customarily make up the second-
ary-school curriculum. Again, it is fortunate that
we *can* get these without hurting the weightier
matters; but most schools, sad to say, pursue the
school studies at the cost of nearly all else.

One further word. The solemn fact that each child
learns what he lives, learns what he accepts as his to act
on, gives specific content to the teacher's moral obligation. We are responsible, so far as taking thought

will affect it, for what our children live. Not that we can compel them to live the way we approve; that would fail. They learn what *they* accept, accept on the inside, not what we compel them to show on the outside. They learn what they internally accept as theirs to live by. We can help, but they ultimately decide what they will build into character.

The modern school is nothing more or less than the honest effort to live up to these things. To call such things "fads and frills" is to make sport of valuation itself; it is to deny the most important things in order that meanwhile we may get the less important. Life, the quality of living, building the quality of life into character—than these the teacher has no greater obligation. These things stand first.

XI

EDUCATION OF ADOLESCENTS IN DEMOCRATIC LIVING*

IN THE light of the discussions given in the chapters on learning, it is easy to see that, if our youth are to learn democracy, they must live democracy. That is, home and school and club life must be run democratically, must afford such a life of acting on thinking, such shared thinking and co-operative acting, as makes abundant use of democratic attitudes and democratic practices. With these principles in mind we are ready to lay down the following criteria for judging the opportunities granted, whether these do or do not make for democracy as our youth live them.

I. Is Purposeful Activity Present and How Intense Is the Interest in It?

If we expect a boy or girl to learn from the activities engaged in, this is the first question we must ask, because this embodies, as we saw earlier in the principles of learning, the prime requisites of efficient learning.

It may be well to insist that no "soft pedagogy" is here contemplated. Purposing and satisfaction are emphasized because in sober fact of science they are necessary; but they are not incompatible with hardness. In fact, exactly contrariwise. Hardness of effort must come from within to meet outside difficulty, else shirking and not

---

* This is a revision, made in 1940, of part of an article which originally appeared in *Religious Education*, June, 1919.

hardness ensues. Purposing contemplates doing something, not merely thinking about it. It is doing that counts in character-building.

II. Is Adequate Provision Made for Wise Guidance?

It is of supreme importance that the right response to a situation be fixed in the child's character. An important part of guidance comes from the tell-tale elements of the situation itself: whether a nail is struck on the head is soon evident. But this is a slow and often-times costly process. The experience of others must be available if damage is to be avoided. An older person properly qualified can with nice tact help the young to purpose more wisely and execute more successfully.

The two foregoing criteria apply to the conditions of learning. We come now to the criteria for democracy. No complete discussion of the meaning of democracy can be given here. Democracy implies, among other things, that there be in matters of conduct the conscious choice on the part of the agent of ends and means in accordance with foreseen and desired good results that are to flow from his conduct. "The conscious choice, on the part of the agent, of ends and means"; but we cannot stop right there. The agent must choose "in accordance with foreseen and desired good results." Good results "are to flow from his conduct." Now, if any wish to ask what is meant by good—if I beg the question here, I plead guilty—I am not going to define the good. But I will say that I have in mind generally the development and expression of personality throughout the social group, and I have in mind activity, the doing of something.

Good lies along these lines. Considering now the principle laid down, as soon as we say conscious choice, we find one of the criteria to judge whether the activity under discussion leads toward democracy. We accordingly lay down as the first criterion on the democratic aspect of our problem:

III. To What Extent Is There Provided the Opportunity for Making Conscious Choice?

If any organization or agency or institution does not provide abundant opportunity for making conscious choice, then, in my judgment, it is not acting along democratic lines. This opposes the autocratic rule of the few from above. It does not deny the rule of the majority, but a majority ought so to act that others will acquiesce of their own reason and choice. This criterion specifically denies mere habituation even in good conduct. This is not to deny that a very young child must begin with mere habituation, but it does deny that the child should continue in mere habituation. Otherwise we are not democratic. Children as they grow older should, in proportion to their maturity, make—under wise guidance—conscious choice of their conduct. Otherwise, even though they be learning to do things that are good, they are not being developed in democracy. This principle opposes, furthermore, indoctrination, because indoctrination is the fixing of the child's choice before he is able to make a choice, so as to prevent him from making a free choice when he has grown older. This first criterion opposes, then, the autocratic rule of the few, mere habituation, and indoctrination. It demands the maximum feasible utilization of purposing by the individuals as individuals, and by the groups as groups of which they as individuals compose the parts.

A second criterion that I draw from the same general principle, the fourth in order, is to ask whether in each case the agent has the opportunity to act from worthy motives, or more generally:

IV. To What Extent Are the Highest Available Motives Utilized?

To go back to the principle, you recall there was to be not only choice, but choice in view of desired good results. Now if our institution or agency puts before young people things to do, but does not provide opportunity to act from worthy motives, we are failing to build the high-grade characters necessary for a real democracy. The criterion contemplates that we will use in each instance the highest motive that will work. This gives us all that is necessary to secure results—practical results if you wish—but it bids us put character results first. The principle even allows punishment, but it reminds us that punishment properly serves to get the individual immediately concerned and others whom he influences to a place where they will act from worthier motives. When then we exert pressure, we do so as effectually as we can to carry all concerned higher up the scale of worthy motives.

Let us now lay down another principle, and draw criteria from it. The notion of democracy demands of each the conscious working in ever-growing relationships for the good of those about us. Each term will repay consideration. The word conscious goes right back to

what we have just been discussing, to criteria III and IV.
The ever-growing relationship means exactly what it
says—working in human relationships that continually
reach out in ever new connections. The last part we are
quite familiar with—for the good of those about us. From
this principle we get three further and final criteria. I
ask first with reference to any series of activities that are
proposed:

**V. To What Extent Is There Present the Opportunity to Develop, in Com-
munity With Others, an Ever-increasing Range of Active Social
Interests?**

The emphasis here is on *interests*—active social interests, an ever-growing range of interests. Without this we
cannot have the ever-growing human relationships called
for by our principle. The question then is: Does our
institution, does our organization, provide abundant opportunity and encouragement for the development, in
company with others, of interests, interests that lead out
into ever new fields of social activity and so bring people
together in ever wider and freer interaction? The next
criterion is a close correlation of this fifth:

Partly as corollary of the preceding, partly as necessary
to its fulfillment, we lay down the sixth criterion:

**VI. To What Extent Is Opportunity Provided to Study the Nature and
Working of Our Social Institutions?**

Clearly, when one speaks of studying our social institutions, a certain emphasis is placed on maturity. So this
criterion would have to be applied according to the maturity of the young people concerned; but there ought
to be some kind of study, certain attitudes built up, even
among the younger adolescents.

For one thing, as the youth grow older they must gain by positive study and discussion ever better insight into social problems and principles. Youth faces now the most serious social problems that any youth have ever faced. For their own sakes now and later they must gain such insight as gives each one a dependable social outlook so that (if it is humanly possible) he may maintain morale even amid great social trials and disappointments. Specific insights will help one also to contribute his part to the democratic solution of our urgent social problems. Along with insight must go also co-operative efforts at making social contributions, as is discussed under the last criterion. Here is the practical welding of insight and self-control we wish to stress. And, finally, it may be added that adequate insight can be got only by studying live-issue problems. Our clubs and schools alike must deal with current controversial issues. On no other basis can proper social intelligence be built or adequate insights achieved.

I should like to emphasize that this sixth criterion calls for the developing of the questioning attitude, the disposition not to swallow things whole as the politicians would like to have us. I was interested this morning to compare headlines with the body of the cablegram. The two didn't fit. I suspected that the man who made the headlines was trying to do our thinking for us and I believed that it was not a democratic procedure. So that, if we want democracy, I should like to insist that we must get our young people to a place where they will not countenance that sort of thing.

VII. To What Extent Is Opportunity Provided for Co-operation to Social Ends in Ever-widening Social Groups?

In the fifth criterion the emphasis was on interests; here it is on co-operation, on the opportunity of co-operating on an ever-widening scale. This seventh criterion means, among other things, the refusal to accept dividing cleavages within the social group. This is a very serious and a very far-reaching corollary. The stress is on refusal to accept dividing cleavages. We cannot forbid them, as intelligent people, to recognize anything that exists, but we must refuse to *accept* cleavages. We must co-operate with ever-widening—not co-operate up to this line and stop—but co-operate with ever-widening social groups and agencies. If one had to choose a single definition of democracy, it would be hard to choose a better than this, co-operation in its broadest sense in ever-widening relationships.

These seven criteria are perhaps not inclusive of all that might be demanded, nor are they altogether mutually exclusive, but I think there is in each an emphasis we need to keep in mind: Intensity of interest in purposeful activity, adequate guidance, conscious choice, utilization of worthy motives, building active social interests, the study of our social institutions, and co-operation with ever-widening groups.

It will be well to ask how some of these criteria correlate. Consider first the bearing of choice as given in the third criterion and guidance as called for in the second. Here is a permanent problem of education. We must allow choice, and we must have guidance. On the one hand, choice and purposing are necessary if the individual is to get into the game for all he is worth. Without choice and purposing there is little learning and growth in character. On the other hand, without guidance our growth may not be in the right direction. What shall we do? An older pedagogy said we could do without the first if only we are strong on the second. A saner view says to get both. He who would guide must so lead that there will be the maximum of purposing by the young, but it must be wise purposing. This points an important lesson. We must have leaders of our adolescents educated, not merely trained. Training is part of education, but not a substitute for it. These leaders must be educated as to where we are going and why, and as to the skills of getting there. The leader is thus responsible for choice and purpose on the one hand as truly as for guidance; because we need both. In my judgment this looks to a profession of leadership in work with adolescents.

Definite difficulties on this question of guidance and choice have been called to my attention. It has been pointed out that there are group leaders who are self-sufficient and autocratic in deciding things for the group under them. There are leaders who do not see why young people are concerned in making decisions, nor do they seem to understand why young people must purpose. Not appreciating the reasons for these, they therefore are not so intelligent as they should be in directing affairs. It was several times pointed out—it might have been pointed out in a large volume—that many high-school teachers have never got this idea at all. Boards of directors, likewise, were said to lay down programs in

utter disregard of choice on the part of those for whom
the program exists.   Such boards of directors are to be
found from time to time wherever there are boards of
directors.   Every institution can show instances.

Closely connected with the foregoing is a twin tendency, especially seen in doctrinal institutions, to treat
young people as mere means to the end of furthering
institutional aims, particularly the perpetuation of
the organizations themselves.   The most flagrant instances are, perhaps, church schools, young people's societies in connection with churches, the formal high
schools, and youth in industry.   The last named is, I
suppose, avowedly selfish; the others not.   Not all church
schools or young people's societies sin in this respect,
certainly not in equal degree.   But the evil is wide-spread.
The formal high school we hope will change under the
influence of a growing democracy.   Indoctrination, however, is fundamentally and essentially undemocratic.   It
intends to anticipate choice.   It inherently uses the individual as a means to an end, and this danger is present
wherever any type of authoritarianism prevails.

The next thing by way of application to which I invite
your attention, is the connection between purposeful
activity and group co-operation, especially as regards character modification.   It has already been emphasized how
purposeful activity supplies the condition of learning.
It is co-operative purposeful activity in group affairs that
has perhaps most to do with building the healthy social
character, with its spirit of give and take, its like-minded-
ness, its tendency to prefer the group and its welfare to
one's private and personal welfare.   This conception

must and will, I believe, make over American education from top to bottom.

By way of contrast consider in connection organized (playground) recreation and the moving picture show. For the former the critics have had great praise. The range of activity is clearly limited, but the character-effect was most highly commended. The moving picture show was severely criticized for the quality of films presented. But as bad in their effects as vicious films may be, it is a more inherent weakness to which I wish to direct attention. With the best of films the moving picture can never be more than a very partial educational agency. The inherent defect is that the spectators are primarily recipients rather than agents. In the playground activities the young act, and most vigorously, together. Hence the social character-effects discussed in the preceding paragraph follow. With the moving picture, however, suppose two hundred or two thousand see the show together. They do not co-operate in any true sense. As a rule they do nothing about what they see. A few ill-mannered may whisper together; the others are more or less conscious that many people are present. At times there may be expressions of common approval, but co-operation there is not, and resulting action but rarely takes place. We can teach some things by means of the moving picture, but the effects seem to me limited to amusement, data of information, and suggestion as to what may later be done. Suppose the suggestions were always good, they would even then be worse than worthless if not followed up and acted out. Much the same can be said of the information. Mere data held in mind are not wisdom. For this must be a working over of information in purpose and effort.

The notion of amusement calls for further remark. America is in danger of thinking that life consists properly of two disparate parts, labor, with the accompanying notion of drudgery, and leisure, with the accompanying notion of having a "good time." So stated, it seems to me almost the most awful mistake that a nation can make. Our industrial system unfortunately has come as near to making us think this way as anything possibly could. It is partly to offset this that I am so insistent on purposeful activity. We want purposeful activity to permeate the work; then work will cease to be drudgery. We want purposeful activity to permeate leisure; then leisure will tend less to harm and more to happiness.

Finally, let it be clearly understood that we are not preparing these boys and girls merely to live after a while. We expect them to live now. This error has been almost universal throughout our past education. So nearly so that we can hardly form a sentence about education that does not imply and incorporate this erroneous conception. We must not think of the child-period as a probationary period for life later on. Our boys and girls must live now. This does not mean that they live merely now, but rather that they are so to live now that they will also live well later on. All schools, both church and lay, seem prone to this error. Education is not to be considered as a mere preparation for life. It is life.

XII

HOW CHARACTER COMES*

Is CHARACTER built or born? Or wherein built and wherein born? If built, by child or adult, how does the building take place?

A mother "successful" with the first child is a staunch advocate of the building theory but when there are three, and little Tom refuses to be built according to plan, the mother says that each is a distinct personality, dating from the beginning. From the very first week Tom would stiffen his backbone to show that he meant to have his own way in this world, and persists so, in spite of determined efforts of both parents.

Are characters then born? Yes and no. Within limits they are born, within limits built. Nature furnishes tendencies and sets limits to possible changes. Nurture chooses from among the tendencies and realizes in greater or less degree the possibilities given at birth. These hereditary tendencies come from the long line of ancestry. In nurture the conscious choice and guidance of adults play a part, but it is the general social environment that on the whole both holds the old and guides the young. Before considering just how these several factors enter, let us consider the matter of learning.

Learning is much more than the acquiring of informa-

---

* Adapted from an article by this title in *The World Tomorrow*, September, 1922.

117

tion; it enters into all man's doings, his inward thoughts and feelings as well as his outward acts. To learn is to get new ways of doing these things. It then refers to changes in any or every kind of conduct. Or, saying it in a slightly different way, learning means a change in us such that different conduct will thereafter come. Since conduct flows from character, it is exactly true that learning means a change in character. Conduct is of the moment; it passes (in a sense) in the doing. Character remains between acts as the abiding tendency to act again. Learning fixes the present conduct in such a way as to bring a change in character, such a change in character as brings thereafter a different conduct. How character comes into being is thus after all exactly a question of how learning takes place. Character is probably the best word to mean the working of the whole person—knowing, feeling, thinking, willing, acting—all. As conduct—the fleeting—includes all of these, so also does character, which abides in and between instances of conduct. (Any use of the word character to mean only moral character, and that as a kind of corrective to the rest of one's being, can only mislead; character is here used to mean "all of our tendencies to behavior of whatever kind, our more settled ways of behaving in every field.")

Since learning changes conduct into character, let us next consider conduct. It is most useful perhaps to think of conduct as a response made to a situation that confronts one. My friend salutes me; I respond, "Good morning." He invites me to join in a speculative business venture; I promptly decline. Three things need here to be distinguished: the situation that stirs me, the response that I make, and the character elements in me that determine my response.

These character elements in me have, we ordinarily say, two sources: nature and nurture, or heredity and environment. That some ways of responding are inherited requires no argument. No child needs to be taught to cry upon feeling pain. He is already provided with that way of behaving. But how to tell his mother some years later that a pin is pricking him—that he must learn. Furthermore, children differ both in what they bring thus with them into the world, and much more in the ease with which they acquire new responses. One learns quickly, another slowly. And there is great difference in ease of learning among different kinds of things. Mary will learn music far more readily than Susan. James will readily learn to "give in to" his mother, but Thomas "just won't learn" this. "Punishment doesn't do any good," his mother says, "he goes on just the same." Here we return to the question as to whether characters are born or built. Under identical treatment James will go through life less "self-assertive" than Thomas, because, since he began life with different native endowments (that is, different capacities to learn on this point), the similar rewards and punishments have different effects upon them. Like forces acting on different situations produce different effects. It is conceivable, if the initial differences were not too great, that different treatment might reverse the bent of nature and James might become the self-assertive one. When no such reversal of native preference is evident, one says that that

particular phase of adult character was "born" in the
person.   The preference was born; but it was later fixed
by favoring circumstances.   Again, nature gives original
tendencies and fixes the limits within which they may be
changed.   A proper scheme of education undertakes to
make such changes as are feasible along the lines approved by the best thought of the time.

We Learn Only Our Responses

Let us next consider how changes are made in one's
ways of behaving; or, in other words, how learning takes
place and so changes conduct.   This matter has been discussed at some length in Chapters VIII and IX.   Here it
will suffice to recall the following:

> We learn our responses—learn them as we accept
> them to act on; and we learn them in the degree that
> we accept them.
> What is learned is therein interwoven, more or less
> fully, with the aggregate of one's manifold abiding
> responses that we call character.

To say that one learns his responses may at first sound
like a truism, which tells us, therefore, nothing helpful;
but this is far from being so, especially when we add the
further words that one learns his responses *as he accepts
them.*   Curiously enough, there are many parents, teachers, and leaders who seem content that children obey
them outwardly, disregarding what really counts: namely
how the children are thinking and feeling inwardly.
Children learn their responses, not as parents and other
elders order, but as the children themselves accept.   It

is what they think (accept) that counts in this matter
of learning. A tired father, irritated by the noise made
by the children, even after mother has spoken, explodes
with: "If you can't keep quiet, you'll go to bed at once.
Do you understand?" The children then keep quiet,
and the father nods to the mother as if to say, "That's
the way to teach them." The children keep quiet, but
what is it they are learning? Are they responding with
consideration for a tired father? Is this what they think
and feel? Is it consideration that they are accepting to
act on? Or are they responding with prudence—prudence
as their response to an angry father? The answer depends on the facts in the particular case, on what response
they actually accept and make to the situation. If they
do in fact think of the father as tired, and, so thinking,
do refrain from noise because they prefer his comfort
to their loud play, then they are responding with consideration and are accepting that to act on. If these
things are so, then they are learning consideration and
are building that into character.

But if they think, "Father is angry, and we'll catch it
if we don't look out," then it is prudence they are accepting to act on, and it is prudence—prudence in the face of
danger—that they are learning and building into character.

As we think further of these things, we see that "as a
man thinketh in his heart, so is he." It is not what the
child does outwardly in answer to commands and threats
that will upbuild his character. It is only as he of himself accepts the better ways as his ways that he builds the
better ways into his character. Indeed, commands and

threats may have just the opposite effect. When the
father scolds them, it may be that some of the older children will see (or think they see) the injustice of his words.
If so, they may respond with thoughts of condemnation.
When such things do happen, there is being built, not
consideration of a tired father, but condemnation of an
unjust father, with the result that that child and that
father are traveling the road that leads to alienation.

It is the fine quality of the child's own thoughts and
feelings that will build a finer quality in him. The part
of parents and other leaders is mainly to encourage and
stimulate the finer thoughts and feelings and then to help
the child really to act them out. It is such things as these
that upbuild character. This is not to deny that parents,
teachers, and other leaders may have occasion at times
to refuse and at other times to order. But those are
emergency measures to prevent worse things. They cannot become the main staple diet of character building.
The main line is at best an indirect way. We work that
the child may in his own heart think and wish the better
things. For he will learn his responses and nothing else,
and these only and exactly as he accepts them.

One significant part of our problem was until recently
not sufficiently considered: namely, the matter of personality adjustment. If any organism is to adjust itself successfully as it faces life's vicissitudes, it must itself be in
good adjustment, and for humans an important factor
in this is the forming of helpful rather than hurtful habits
and attitudes. It is this fact that puts personality into the
discussion of character building.

Most maladjustment, it appears, begins in the early

years of life. Often it arises out of some sense of insecurity which may manifest itself in various ways, such
as excessive shyness, unwillingness to try new things, or
in such opposites as excessive loudness and other demands
to be the center of attention. We who are concerned with
youth must be sensitive to the maladjustments already
present when we appear on the scene. Some will be so
serious that in them we must be guided by expert advice.
But, for most of the youth under our care, wise treatment
by us will help the lesser instances of maladjustment and
avoid starting other difficulties.

Each person has, we may say, an upper limit to the
amount of difficulty he can cope with successfully. One
may fail to attain his end and still so digest his failure as
to come off personally the victor. For example, one may
so study the reasons of his failure that he now yearns for
another challenge. That man's failure has helped him;
he has digested the experience. He is now a stronger man
both in knowledge and in "will." But another may be
so discouraged by his failure that he refuses to think
openly or willingly about the causes of failure. Instead,
he broods over the pains of defeat. If the like recurs
soon enough and often enough, this person will build a
chronic sense of failure. He will not exert himself as
others do; yet he is unable to accept the situation. That
others try and succeed galls him; yet he seems helpless
to try. He has built an "inferiority complex."

There are other hurtful attitudes that, following undigested failures, may similarly become chronic. One
person will thus develop a chronic "grouch" from successive undigested instances of resentment. Another will

similarly develop a "morbid conscience." Another may "escape" from the hard realities of ordinary life into day-dreaming, where he can fix both conditions and outcomes so as there to play the hero in a way denied him in the actual world. Still another may refuse to tell himself honestly the difficult factors that he in fact sees before his very eyes: we say of him that he "refuses to face reality." Many and sad are the "escape mechanisms" that failing people devise in the vain effort thus to save themselves.

The conclusion for us is that we must sense such tendencies before they become fixed—and their possibility even before they start. Probably our best single device is to help any doubtful youth attempt at first less difficult feats but be sure he succeeds at them. If this can happen often enough with gradually increasing difficulties, we can reasonably hope to build up a better morale. And all the while we shall cultivate the practical study of each successive situation so as to build a morale founded on intelligent methods of attack. It is acting on thinking—insistent acting on carefully directed thinking—that is the underlying principle upon which we must act.

Before we conclude, it may be well to consider various matters often brought forward when character building is under discussion.

Some "modern-minded" people seem to think that a person's character is made up of many separate habits or traits, which can be built one at a time, each one without much reference to the others. Those who take this position are likely to leave thinking out of account, and hold that character building is exactly habit or trait building, adding one habit at a time to what has gone before, as "leg over leg the dog went to Dover."

But thinking is a highly necessary part of character. Only as a person has built it into his character to think before he acts does he have a properly working character. Habits will not as a rule work well unless thinking is present to direct them intelligently in the particular situation. Good thinking also helps us, whether young or old, to profit by our experience, to be more sensitive to the situation, so that we act more suitably next time.

It may help us to look at another instance of conduct to see how thinking must be an essential part of good character. Take the quality of kindliness—a virtue that all will approve—and ask how the process of being kindly goes on or fails to go on. We wish particularly to see how thinking and habit enter together when one really does act in kindly fashion.

A father just leaving for his office refuses permission to his nine-year-old son to go on a hike after school because he wishes him to run an errand. The matter seemed small to the father, but he was troubled to learn later from his wife that the boy had cried a good deal over his disappointment, the hike being a special one with the boys. If this father had but known how much it meant to the boy, he would gladly have found another time for the errand. Does, now, this father act in kindly fashion? In general intent, yes. In this particular instance, no— he failed to be as kindly as he might because he failed to make inquiry before he decided. If he had thought to inquire, he would have seen the situation differently and so would have acted differently.

Any lack of kindliness in this instance seems then due to lack of thinking, and this in turn perhaps to lack of a well-made habit of talking things over with the boy before deciding on his requests. Probably if the boy should make another request the next day, the father would inquire before he decided. He might still refuse, but only after he had pointedly thought over what was involved. And if the father continues thereafter to think thus more fully before he decides on such matters, he will have grown by that much in effectual kindliness in dealing with his son. In other words, his behavior, in this respect, will be more intelligently directed and he will therefore be more adequately kind.

Still again, many think of character building as a matter of adding a new course in school, somewhat as a high school may introduce debating, or a study of modern economic problems, into its curriculum. Those who separate character from mind, making two things of them, are rather likely—as they get troubled about "our degenerate days"—to wish schools to introduce a course in character building, and they somehow expect teachers to "teach" children "how to behave" either by requiring them to memorize such things as Collier's Code of Morals or the Ten Commandments or by learning "instinctive obedience." Others will take counsel of those who stress the separate-habit idea and seek through teachers (or, more often, through boys' clubs and the like), to have the young people practise specified habits or do "good deeds," and get stars or buttons or badges according to reports handed in by the children and countersigned, it may be, by careless and complacent parents. But any such procedure is a snare and a delusion. The character of these young people is, as we have seen, being built day by day, hour by hour, as they live through the situations of their daily lives and make decisions in connection. To expect to counteract that constant building successfully in an hour or two a week is at the best to expect something highly improbable; at the worst, to bring results in the highest degree undesirable. Character building is no get-rich-quick affair. It requires every day and all the time.

Punishment, Obedience, and Coercion

Many ask about punishment. Does the statement that our part is only indirect mean that parents and teachers shall never use punishment? It is a complex problem. If baby pulls things off the table, we can by consistent negative conditioning teach her not to do so, and she will learn. This is not punishing her in the old sense because she has done wrong and wrong demands punishment. Rather is it a positive program of conditioning one too young to learn by seeing and understanding results. With older children, punishment is less valuable. Here the child's thinking is active and inclusive, and the boy or the girl may outwardly learn the wisdom of obeying but inwardly may be building antagonistic feelings that may later work most disastrously.

And what about obedience? Ought not the child to learn obedience? Obedience is a very handy thing to have around the house and probably should be sought —intelligently—from early childhood. But let us make no mistake. It is intelligently self-directed characters

that we are, as a long term effort, trying to help build.
Many parents of an earlier day preferred obedience to
thinking in children. Two opposed dangers here
threaten. One is that the child may become hurtfully
docile, unable, and unwilling to make decisions for himself. Such a child is easily led astray when the time comes
to go away to college or to the great city. The other
danger is that the child may become rebellious, and so
again fail to become adequately self-directing. Many
"modern" parents go to the third extreme of spoiling the
children when they are young and have "cute" ways of
saying and doing what they please. At first, if the child
be thoughtfully led, he is naturally obedient—he knows
little else to do. This early stage should be utilized as
scaffolding for building ever more thoughtful consideration of the rights and feelings of others. In this way obedience to parents yields gradually to obedience to the reasonable demands of the situation.

Some will ask whether coercion may not be properly
used to make a child try something at which he could
succeed, where success will almost surely be a matter of
later satisfaction. If we so apply our coercion as not to
arouse too violent opposition, we may perhaps wisely use
this as a last resort. But, as before intimated, to use
such coercion usually or even frequently is likely to do
more harm than good. When such coercion does succeed it is because it leads quickly enough to gratifying
success, so that this will supply the further motivation
needed. This suggests that a better way as a rule is to
rely upon an easy rather than a repellent start.

It may be added that life itself does much if not most

of the needed teaching along the line of character building. The child is naturally and incessantly active. The
environment gives him stuff with which to be active. It
does more; it teaches him. It acts selectively. When he
touches a hot coal, it teaches him by the acute attendant
annoyance not to do so again. Grandmother gives him
sugar, the attendant satisfaction sends him back to grandmother again and again. He pulls Jane's hair; Jane and
mother teach him not to do so. When he gets older, he
attempts to defy the other boys, but they are too strong
for him. In one way or another they break him in to
the established ways of behavior among boys. In the end
he strongly approves and helps similarly to break others
into the established order.

Now character is thus being built all the while. The
child of any age has his own tendencies stirring to inces-
sant action. The environment, physical and social, calls
these out, furnishes more or less adequately the means
of expression, and by the always attendant satisfaction or
annoyance tends to fix in him appropriate ways of behavior. Of well nigh supreme importance in this connection are the ways of behavior that society has evolved,
customs imbedded in the habits of the members of society. These make insistent demands on the growing
individual! Deviation from them is in some way or other
punished; accord with them, rewarded. The aggregate
of his built-up responses, duly interwoven, constitute his
character.

We may then draw these conclusions: First, as to
whether character is built or born. The rough tendencies with their varied comparative strengths are given at

birth, but these are shaped within very wide limits by
the later life. Nurture has its very important part to
play. Secondly, there is the question as to who builds
the character, adult or child. It is the child's own responding that must build his character. The adult is
outside, but not so far outside as to have no influence.
By stimulating to this or that, by giving or withholding
opportunities, by influencing (within limits) the satisfactions or annoyances felt—herein may the adult so influence the child's conduct as materially to affect his character. *But the part of the adult is forever indirect;* it is
the child who actually and finally builds his own character. It is a sobering fact that we have far more certain
possibilities for evil than we have for good. We can
almost certainly ruin the child's character. We cannot,
with anything like equal certainty, direct it as we would.

How then is good character best built? Surround the
child with an environment rich in stimulation and possibilities. Particularly must it be rich in social contacts.
Encourage him according to his age, tastes, and capacities to engage in activities that challenge his efforts. Let
many activities be purposes shared with others so that
co-operation is necessary. Let there be present and available wise guidance in the person of elders who know
fruitful lines of growth. In the multitudinous social contacts there will inevitably arise situations of social stress.
Under wise guidance the group should be led to see the
issues involved and conclude as to a just disposition of
the dispute. Such a group-conclusion no individual will
permanently dispute. To defy his group seldom satisfies.
In the end he will accept. The wisdom of the race has

thus been accepted by these children—under effective guidance—and embodied into their characters. In such a school as this will the race experience and the necessary rules of learning function hand in hand. As age comes on, situations of increasing complexity arise, but the process remains essentially the same. The resulting character is the correlative of life itself. The wisdom of the ages present in the teacher guides the process along lines approved by the experience of the race. The resulting learning enters continuously into character. So is character built.

XIII
HONORS AND AWARDS*

IT IS character and character building that here demand
our interest and emphasis. Our question is as to the
effect of honors and rewards on the making of character.
Do honors and rewards build desirable character, or do
they secure merely certain outward observances and this
only for a while? The question is complex and knotty.
Otherwise it had been solved long ago, for the problem
is an old one. We must examine carefully the bases of
character making in order to see how such artificial in-
centives as rewards and honors do act. At the outset one
word of warning is necessary. Strictly speaking, no one
can build character in another. Each must build his
own character. The part of all teachers, although real, is
always indirect and only indirect.

The Essence of Character

How shall we conceive character so as to get light on
its building? The answer is clear. Science and common
sense agree. The essence of character is the crystallized
tendency of conduct to repeat itself. This includes
habits of thinking and feeling as truly as habits of more
obvious acting. And the organization is itself simply
other habits. Of course, with our many habits, some

---

* A revision made by the author for this work from an article that
appeared in *The Womans Press*, August, 1924.

leading in one direction and others in other directions, there are often conflicts. Just here is the need for organization. Character as an aim demands, then, not only the individual habits and the organization of these into larger and larger systems of habits, but also thinking to adapt these as may be needed in novel situations. Let no one suppose that life merely repeats itself. Among the most useful habits are those for careful thinking by which we better take care of new situations. The essential element of character thus is habit of all kinds: thinking, feeling, outward behavior.

But a moral habit is more than outward behavior. To be moral, the inner attitude must go along with outward behavior. Make no mistake, however: Inner attitude is just as truly habit as outward behavior. And we who are concerned with the best possible character must be very sure of both aspects of conduct. To be content with inner attitude is to be merely sentimental. It is faith without works, empty. To be content with mere outward and formal behavior and indifferent to the accompanying spirit is to build an essentially immoral character. We must have both fitly joined together, the inner attitude and the outward behavior. This is moral habit.

And the efficient moral character is, as already suggested, more than a set of fixed-in-advance habits, which, like so many push-buttons, bring forth the right response as the occasions present themselves. Many typical situations do repeat themselves, to be sure; and appropriate responses to these should be reduced to dependable habits. But life is vastly more complex than that. No moral character can deal adequately with the novel and uncertain situations of life on the basis of fixed habits alone.   More is needed.   Conscious deliberation is an absolutely essential ingredient of the effective moral character, at times to decide on the true character of the confronting situation, at other times to decide how to deal with such a situation.   This moral deliberation can proceed only on the basis, first, of foreseeing reasonably the many varied results of alternative proposed lines of conduct and, secondly, of weighing these opposed consequences in terms of the values respectively at stake. Nothing short of continual acting on thinking, day after day, can build the requisite knowledge of probable outcomes or the needed system of values.   This acting on thinking is at the same time the best way of building the better defined habits.   On both counts, the efficient moral character must be a thoughtful and intelligent character.

Character Building

How, then, is the desired moral character to be built; and what if any part in the process have such tangible rewards and honors as buttons and badges?   The foundations of character building are elsewhere discussed at length (see the preceding chapter).   For present purposes, those discussions may be summed up in the two following statements, both simultaneously true:

1. A person learns what he lives.   He learns each of his responses *as* he accepts it, and he learns it in the degree that he counts the matter important to him.

2. In any life situation, a person will (1) note and distinguish in that situation what seems to him im-

portant; and (2) what he thus notes he will relate
with other things either present or otherwise in
mind so as best to take account of what seems to him
at stake.   (3) What is thus related—be it idea or
feeling or impulse, or all together—he will accept
(in some sense) to act on according to the importance
he attaches to it.   (4) What he thus accepts, he learns,
that is he builds it, as accepted, at once into character, there to enter appropriately into further behavior.

In the light of these principles what shall we say about
the use of honors and awards in our dealing with boys
and girls?

A true instance comes to mind. A few days ago a
mother came to the writer with this problem. Her son,
a Boy Scout Cub, wished her to sign a statement certifying
that he had learned to brush his teeth. She declined on
the grounds that he does not brush his teeth with any
regularity. He insisted that his next button depended
on the signature, and that all the other mothers had
similarly signed. What, now, did the button do for this
boy? Did it teach him to brush his teeth? Apparently
not. But that's not all. That boy seemed to be learning
that certificates need not, either necessarily or properly,
fit the facts; and that buttons might properly follow a
false statement of facts. Nor could his mother prevent
these bad learnings, for *he* learned what *he* accepted.
It appears that he was willing to learn the false use of
certificates and that the button system as used brought
about this result, not only with him but with the other

boys involved. This use of buttons actually taught positive immorality.

Let us examine what might be thought of as a more
typical case—one that seems to bring out better the essential working of specific awards. A girl is trying to get a
badge for "helpfulness to mother." We will suppose
that she does in fact perform the stipulated acts of "helpfulness" so that the mother can and does properly certify
to them. What then has the girl learned? Has she built
the habit of being "helpful" to mother?

From the principles of learning summarized above,
it is clear that what the girl learns will depend on what
goes on in her mind and heart as she performs the acts.
And what does go on in the girl's mind might vary over
a wide range, from an almost total absorption in badge-
getting (with a correlative absence of regard for mother)
at the one extreme, to the almost total absorption in
mother (with correspondingly little regard for the badge)
at the other. The nearer she comes to the first, the nearer
she is to learning just plain selfishness coupled perhaps
with a little increased skill in performing the deeds. The
nearer she comes to the other, the more unselfish she is
learning to be, but the less influence the badge is having.

The doubtful question is whether one would start in
with eyes fixed on the badge and end up with eyes better
fixed on mother. The hope of badge advocates is that
this would happen to the girl, that she will, in order to
perform the stipulated "helpful acts," have to think about
mother and how to help mother so that some habit of
thoughtfulness may remain after the badge is awarded.
That this may happen cannot be denied; that it will

happen cannot be asserted. The most we can say is that the more the girl thinks of the badge, the less likely is she learning to be thoughtful of mother. The question, then, naturally arises as to whether the badge is not more likely to distract attention from mother than otherwise; whether, after all, the group leader had not better start with mother than with badge.

In this connection, some may raise the question of group approval. Cannot mother and the other members of the family so approve the "helpful" acts, even though begun selfishly, as to cause the girl's attention to shift gradually from the selfish interest in the badge to the unselfish interest in mother and helpfulness to her? This again is possible. Wise approval is a very helpful factor in such matters. Wise guidance can help direct the girl's thinking to mother's heavy work, her many cares, and her none-too-strong physique, and these may so appeal that the girl, although hitherto thoughtless, now does consider her mother and how she may lighten rather than increase mother's burden. If so, and the girl does so really consider her mother and does seek opportunities to help, then we can be fairly sure that she will learn to be more thoughtful. But again the question comes as to what the badge did, and why use it.

There is one final consideration before we conclude the discussion. So far we have spoken as if a person always has just one satisfaction in doing any given thing. Such singleness of heart is rare. Almost always there are various satisfactions. Even the mother who clothes her baby is influenced by what others will think of the clothes as truly as by the needs of warmth and other comforts.

And so it will be with any girl or boy member of any group; rewards and honors join with jolly companionship, approval of leader and group, the fun of action, the approval of conscience, to make up the actual effective satisfaction in whatever is undertaken. This complexity lessens the proportion of responsibility we accord to rewards and honors; but whatever part they play they are to be judged as good or bad in their effects according to the considerations urged above.

The Use of Rewards and Honors

What rôle, then, have rewards and honors in character building?

1. In the degree that our young people seek any reward purely for the sake of the reward and think only of it and practise thus only selfish satisfactions, in that degree does the system of offering rewards build not moral character but selfishness. To use rewards and honors must be counted as immoral unless in fact the original satisfaction of the external reward gradually gives way to an inner satisfaction in the activity itself or in the helpful effects of the activity on others. To use rewards and honors simply in and of themselves cannot be defended as a means of building desirable characters.

2. If the attention of the young people is not on the reward itself, but on the approval of others won by the reward, we have probably taken a step upward in the scale of morals. But even here there is a question. If the approval received is merely self-centered, we have progressed but little, if any, above plain selfishness.

3. If the rewards and honors are used, like scaffolding

in housebuilding, as temporary devices to get desirable action started so that we may later remove the scaffolding and leave the house standing in its own strength, then we may say that the results are good. But the test is: Can the scaffolding be removed? Will the building stand alone? Are we in fact building positive interests that no longer demand or wish rewards or honors?

4. There are certain incidental effects of rewards that may be positively good. The definite suggestions of desirable activities may be of great assistance. A mere trial of these will often suffice to bring inherent satisfaction and so add an abiding interest to life. The possibility thus of increasing the interests of our young people is most commendable. Accompanying these is the matter of standards. The definite directions for judging what is done may be of great value in building useful standards of excellence. Increased interests and higher standards are most desirable features in every character.

The Dangers of Rewards and Honors

But there are certain dangers that should be kept in mind:

1. The untrained leader may easily confuse values, and fail to see that the rewards are good only as they make themselves unnecessary. Much harm is possible here.

2. There is always the danger that any satisfaction from low motives will fasten low motives. And low motives often reach out; where the satisfaction is merely in outward signs, there is often temptation to adopt more or less dishonest measures. This danger is always present

where the sign rather than the substance is the moving cause of action.

3. The definite concreteness of reward may actually interfere with the satisfaction of the good activity on its own account. We are all, youth and adult alike, easily led to ignore the less tangible, if a more tangible is at hand and available.

4. Even if the leaders understand that the reward is only a temporary device to be gradually retired from conscious thought, the shift in satisfaction is not always easy to effect. To succeed requires on the part of the leader a nice skill both in judgment and in human dealings, and the presence of definite machinery for awarding honors adds a further difficulty. A boy or girl may be just ready to forget self and reward and begin to think of helping others, when here comes the button or badge to recall the mind from others to self. The more fixed and inflexible the machinery, the more difficult to think it away.

5. A final danger is that the attention of leaders themselves will, by the system of obvious rewards, be distracted from studying the inherent rewards and satisfactions of healthy social living. Both rewards and punishments may be necessary in life as a last resort; but to keep either in the foreground of thought is to show a distrust in humanity and a lack of faith in life itself. The principal objection to buckeyes as cures for rheumatism is not that a buckeye carried in the pocket will hurt the carrier, but that it serves as a distraction from a real search for real causes. So, in general, whenever we are content with less

than the best possible, we fail to seek what seeking might
find.

The conclusion of the whole matter seems thus to be
that rewards and honors may be used as temporary devices in character building provided they are so understood and are soon discarded accordingly. Otherwise
they may become positively immoral. But at best they
represent a mistrust in the power of the good life to afford
real satisfaction and to win its own way. Why not, as
most of the organizations have done, try the real thing—
the healthy life itself? It seems, in fact, to work best.
Why use the artificial and doubtful when we have available all the possible richness of life itself?

XIV
MY CHILD AS A PERSON *

"I WISH the best possible for my child, but often I neither know what is best nor how to secure what I believe to be best." Thus many a parent feels, and perhaps increasingly so in recent years. Here we are to consider only one phase of the problem, the child as a person and, more particularly, how the child may become more of a person or more fully a person. These words, "more of a person," may sound strange. How shall we understand them?

Consider the saying, "Man is an animal"; and the further saying, "Only a human can be a person." To be a person points then beyond the "mere animal" to something that the mere animal has not or at most has only in lesser degree. We must not here repeat the old mistake of seeing in man two distinct natures joined together. For best opinion now counts that man is a whole and that in his every act all parts of this whole co-operate. But the matter of degree is a fact of nature easily seen. When we contrast stone, tree, dog, and man, there is in the dog clearly more of life, more aliveness, more liveliness than in the tree, and still more of these in man. If the tree and the stone are alike in some things, in weight for instance, they still differ greatly. And the dog differs

---

* Prepared for Vol. XI of *The New Wonder World*, J. R. McGaughy, editor. Geo. L. Shuman & Co., 1932.

from the stone more than does the tree, and man much
more yet. It is this increasing quality in life, in fullness
and variety of life, that here concerns us, this something
of which the dog has more than the tree and the man
more than the dog. In this greater and richer life we
approach nearer to seeing what the person is.

But someone may ask what about this "more of a person or more fully a person"? I see that the dog differs
in this fact and quality of life more from the stone than
the tree does, and man still more, but where is "the more
of a person"? To answer this, suppose we consider another series, a baby one day old, a boy six years old, a
youth of eighteen, and a man of forty, and, to make the
discussion easier, let us suppose that each of these is a
fine specimen for his age. Are there any differences?
What are the chief differences? Bodily differences are
clear. Mentally, the youth, we are told, can learn better
than the boy, and both better than the baby. And in
this learning, the youth is abler than the boy even where
their experiences have been the same; the youth can solve
more difficult problems. As for the youth and the man,
it appears to be true that where their experiences are
about the same they learn about equally well, both in
point of difficulty and otherwise.

But as we think of "more of a person," we are concerned with something beyond just body and learning
ability. This increasing aliveness or growing fullness
and richness of life seems to be closely allied with the use
made of one's talents and opportunities. To bring this
out more clearly, let us consider the boy and let us imagine a second boy of the same age equal at birth in mind

and body with the first, but one who somehow has misused his possibilities.

How does the "more of a person" show itself in the one boy rather than the other? How will the two boys differ? Chiefly perhaps in three respects: in "disposition," in interests, and in their actual working minds. In disposition, the worse boy may be emotionally ill-balanced, spoiled, demanding much attention, easily irritated, quarrelsome with other children, given to tantrums with his parents. Also, in demanding attention to himself, he is likely to resort to increasingly annoying measures until he gets attention even if this be punishment. Or this boy may be emotionally ill-balanced in quite a different way: very shy, a "sissy"—afraid to play with other boys, studious perhaps, but a day-dreamer, possibly the pet of an unwise teacher, but despised by the other boys. He may be the darling of his mother, who comforts him when he seems unable to face life as do the other children. There are, of course, many different ways in which a boy may go wrong. It is interesting, too, that we can describe shortcomings better than excellencies. We have a better set of terms, especially some newer terms, for shortcomings; but it is not so easy to describe excellencies, partly because we are not so well agreed on what is good. Even to this day some parents and teachers like and approve the shy, studious day-dreamer—he is "so good," "so obedient," and "gives so little trouble." But more and more we are asking what kind of future will come out of it and more and more we are seeing that the future is not good for the child who withdraws from life as it is in order to live more happily in his dreamland.

The danger is that he will withdraw more and more from life as it is until he can no longer "face reality." This state of affairs is much more to be feared than many kinds of more positively disagreeable behavior. Some kinds of "bad" boys are much healthier personalities than some "good" boys.

The more fortunate boy is then harder to describe, but we must make the effort. We are seeking to find out what it is to be "more of a person." The more fortunate boy is on the whole sweeter tempered, though he can get angry; but in both moods he is more reasonable. Play means much to him—especially with other boys, but also with girls. In whatever he is doing he expects to be treated fairly and for one of his age he has pretty clearly in mind what fairness demands, not only from the others to him, but also—though less clearly—from him to them. He may at times pout, but it is generally for a reasonable complaint and even then seldom for long. He seldom harbors grievances. At times he seems a bit too argumentative over his rights; but even so he learns, and the next time he will likely see more justly. He enjoys praise, but he does not demand too much attention. In fact, he gives himself now more and more to what he is about, with less thought of himself in connection with what he is doing. He is on good terms with both father and mother and enjoys engaging in enterprises with them, but he has ideas of his own and feels that they should be considered. His parents approve this growing independence, but at times are troubled by his over-insistence on his own point of view. He is generally obedient and trustworthy, but needs help to clarify and maintain standards.

One marked characteristic of the more fortunate boy is the growing range of his interests, and also his giving of himself to these more heartily and more absorbedly than formerly. Although he shows this growing attention and persistence, he can still shift his interest readily —too readily, his parents sometimes think—if something new comes up. He asks many questions, good ones, too, for his age. In fact this is one of the best signs of his growth, that he now asks more and better questions than last year, and also that he shows more desire to answer his own questions and more ingenuity in finding good answers. He likes also to visit and examine new things that he has heard about. He is keen to handle each new thing or otherwise to look closely into it until he understands it to his satisfaction. Sometimes he insists overmuch on knowing what is beyond him, but a further sign of achieved growth is in the increasing depth of his understanding. He goes now deeper down in understanding things. What he has learned shows, both in the better questions that he can ask and in the better quality of work that he does whether anybody is looking or not. He has higher standards. He shows, too, greater resources and greater skill in almost all that he undertakes, but even so, he sometimes attempts more than he can finish. In fact, unwise attempts seem at times his greatest fault; but he appears to be improving in this respect.

To sum up, the worst things perhaps to be found in the less fortunate boy are his lack of emotional stability, his lack of willingness to deal patiently with life as it is—two ways perhaps of describing the same shortcoming. He will not face life as evenly or as fruitfully as he might. He refuses to look squarely and evenly at the situation as he does see it or could see it; and, refusing thus, he easily gets into a rage. Or even worse, refusing to face reality squarely, he creates a dream world and tries to get from it the satisfaction which he is not brave enough to attempt to derive from the real world. And the worst about each of these shortcomings is the future to which it naturally leads.

In contrast, the best things to be found in the more fortunate boy have to do with the quality of his present life, in that they mean happiness now and promise well for the future. First, in particular, this boy is emotionally balanced as he faces difficulty or defeat. What he sees, he looks at squarely—on his level—in order to see better; and he tries bravely to manage what he sees. If he fails at first, he tries again, only more carefully. If he fails finally, he does not get into a pet, but still— always on his level—looks carefully into the cause of his failure and learns from it. Seldom does he yield to rage or pretend that he sees what is not there. All this, of course, is on his level. To us, his seeing may at times seem pathetically short and weak. You or I would often see far more and far better than he, and, if we are not wise, we may short-circuit his efforts by telling him too soon or otherwise hurtfully what we see. But the important thing is not so much what he *now sees,* as the way in which *he* tries to see and work and how *he* profits by failure. It is what *he* is learning mainly in managing himself and in his attacks on problems and situations that counts. It is this that promises growth for the future. What we should wish is to cultivate *his* disposition to attempt bravely, look squarely, and then *himself* profit by the experience. In the degree that these be attained, the other things needed will come in due time. In such ways as these does this boy approach to that "more of a person" which we seek.

It may appear that in our attention to these two boys we have forgotten the youth and the man. How do they come into the picture? How does the youth differ from the boy? Or, perhaps better, how has the promising boy grown into a promising youth? What of the fulfilment and what of the further promise?

The youth differs from the boy chiefly in the degree to which he has grown through his ever-widening and more varied experience. There is more content to his life and greater complexity to his thought, his feelings, and his procedures. His character and his disposition should still be to face his experience bravely and truthfully with himself. Many parents, fearful as to possible outcomes, will discourage the youth from asking difficult questions. There is great danger in such a procedure. If success crowns such parental efforts at suppression and the youth does not face his questions, he may grow not to question. Many children in conservative homes do so cease to question. A stupid conformity has then resulted to reduce by so much the youth's thinking throughout life and to add one more to the ranks of that stubborn and unreasoning conservatism that only too often provokes a more violent reaction in others. If the youth does knowingly set his questions aside, and grows so to do, a certain blasé cynicism easily results. "Why be interested in anything? Why get excited? Be above it." Such a result helps neither him nor the world. On the other hand, the youth's questions may in appearance be set aside but only to be discussed not openly but covertly, with rejection of parents as confidants or guides. This again helps neither him nor the world. The fortunate youth builds on the boy's foundation. Though new and perplexing experiences confront him, he still faces them bravely and squarely to learn from them and build himself stronger and better in the attempt. As hard as it may be for parents and teachers to accept it, the best that can come as the boy grows into the youth and the youth becomes the man is the ever-firm grip that the individual holds on himself as he learns to face the ever-new questions that arise. In the long run it is not so much what answer is now reached—important as that may seem and in fact may be. The important thing is that each one build—each age on its own level —a firm and honest bravery of attack with a growing, just reliance on the methods of attack and a growing, proper criticism of the success attained. If the self can be well and honestly integrated on the basis of a square and unflinching attack with an ever-growing technique and procedure—if these things can be, we have again the best promise for the future.

The youth then will have more interests. The content of any one interest will be deeper in significance. And deeper inquiries will accordingly arise. Where the boy wished to understand the more obvious things of the world about him, the youth will wish a deeper "why" into social and moral life. The widening range of the youth's interests will join him now more closely with other people in society, while certain specially growing concerns will separate him from the mass and lead him into his coming profession.

Possibly the chief difference between the youth and the boy is the matter of degree in thinking. The youth raises more questions because his wider knowledge shows more conflicts. He has learned, too, to make a more conscious effort to look more widely about and deeper down before he decides. The man will think of the youth as still impulsive and so he is; but in comparison with the boy the youth thinks more and better. He looks further into the future; he takes more things into account, and he takes them better into account as he makes up his mind. Moreover, he thinks more about the process of this thinking; he is coming to be a more conscious judge of his own and other people's success in thinking. This better thinking holds for him just as truly in the moral realm as in the intellectual and practical. Where his thinking is bad it is likely to be because his experience is small. Or it may well be because the people about him are not concerned to apply criticism in their thinking. Always we grow more surely when those about us hold up high standards.

As we compare the youth with the man, two things stand out. The man has an occupation that takes his dominant attention, and he has achieved a much wider and better integrated outlook on life. The youth is more often discouraged. Life appears dark. Others do not yet accept him. He does not himself know what he can do, and he does not know what to believe. The man has found out, within limits, what he can do; and he has achieved an outlook that gives him on the one hand a poise and balance in life and on the other—as he sees it—a cause worthy of his best efforts. To have found one's work, to have struck one's true stride, to have achieved an ever-growing, integrating outlook on life— these are life's great achievements.

With the main outlines now before us, what do we conclude is that "more of a person" that we sought at the beginning, and how shall we as parents help our children progressively to achieve it?

Let us first, in summation, recall the quality and content of life. The dog we saw lives more fully than the tree; there is in him more of life to live, more different ways in which to live, more of the quality of enjoyment (so we believe) in what is lived. But if the dog is thus superior to the tree, man in this respect is far superior to both. And similarly, the boy here greatly surpasses the baby; the youth surpasses the boy; and the man should surpass the youth. It seems true, at least in some respects, that childhood and youth have a certain advantage in freshness and vigor of reaction—this is but right. Life at each stage is life in its own right and has its peculiar enjoyments, but increasing experience should bring range and inner distinctions and accumulated insights. Then, to live more in the wider range of achieved experiences, to live at any one time more through a growing experience, to see and feel thus more of actual experiencing, to see and feel more of significance along more lines—wherever these things take place, there life is richer, there the person is himself rich. **This** is one aspect of what it means to be "more of a person."

But there is something more. The person consciously directs his own life. The tree has life and is thus, in a very limited sense, self-directing. The dog has much more of life and in much greater measure directs it. But only man in any full sense directs his several acts in criticized knowledge of what they mean. Man alone acts with conscious, criticized intent. The babe lives vigorously, but, as we know, his life is largely directed for him. The boy is by contrast much more highly self-directing. The youth, however, sees more than the boy and can thus direct his life more intelligently than can the boy. The man sees still more and can still more intelligently and defensibly direct his life. And there is no end to it: Each one can in this regard keep on growing indefinitely. This ever-growing, intelligent self-direction of life in the light of increasing insight and foresight, this taking ever more into account and better, this is perhaps the main sign and evidence of growth as we further define what we mean by the "more of a person."

But there is still more. We may repeat the last thought with emphasis on the responsible acceptance of consequences. A person, in the degree that he acts in any full sense, assumes responsibility for what he does. With a slave, for example, it is different. Plato called a slave an animated tool, because as a slave he accepts his purposes from another. His master uses him as he might a tool. Acting as a slave, he does not carry responsibility for what he does. Any person, in the degree that he is a person, forms his purposes, not arbitrarily from whim or mere prior-formed wish, but only after conscious effort to see and value all the pertinent consequences of his proposed course. In like degree does such a person consciously accept responsibility for the consequences of his act. So to act and so to grow becomes then the moral definition of the "more of a person."

We are now ready to bring together in one focus the various things to be included in the phrase "more of a person, or more fully a person."

First is emotional stability, the integrated personality. This we saw at an early stage as the better six-year-old increasingly faced his life difficulties—"faced reality" on his level—neither in anger at his lack of power nor in cowardly retreat into a dream world, but (to continue with our adult language) in a reasonable effort to do his best with a reasonable willingness to draw appropriate lessons from any outcome, whether of success or failure. We saw the same emotional stability, now grown older, still holding under the fires of adolescence and the same taking on yet further development in the man's ever-growing but still ever-stable outlook on life, an outlook both stable and growing because it is based not on dogmas counted as settled, but rather on methods of study, themselves growing, always available for attack on life's unending stream of novelly developing situations. Such an emotional stability, ever-growing both in external purview and in internal coherence, forms the necessary foundation as we continue to seek the ever "more of a person."

It is the way in which the child meets and grapples with the difficulty that counts, not so much whether he succeeds in what he set out to do as how he carefully tries and how he feels about it afterwards. If he tries faithfully, thinks it through, looks squarely at things, sees how things turn out and why—if he does these things as best he can and does not get angry or try to evade issues, then he is growing and will grow into "more of a person." This growing will thus come about just as surely as a stone turned loose will fall. This is how your child can grow into becoming ever "more and more of a person."

"But what can I do? Where do I come in?" the parent will anxiously ask. The answer is clear. Your part is always indirect. You can directly hurt, but only indirectly can you help. And this is so, because it is what your child himself does that counts here; most of all is it what he does on the inside that counts in building him into "more of a person."

Your child must "try faithfully," but if you *make* him try he may try only on the outside where you can see. It is the way he tries inside that counts. Many parents refuse to see this and they sometimes storm and threaten. This is very dangerous. It is a good way in which to build emotional instability in your child. And here appears perhaps the greatest of possible demands on the parent. If the parents are not emotionally stable, either as they deal with each other before the child or as either deals directly with the child, then the child is in great danger of becoming emotionally unstable himself.

What I can do then to help my child must be by way of giving him a chance to have varied experiences and aiding him to face both faithfully and patiently various problems as they arise, and this in such manner as to learn from the experience whatever it has to teach. One way to help him is to give him a good chance to live, opportunity to play—and later to work—with others near his own age without too much interference from the outside. This is the basis of all else. Without this we can have little hope. But more is needed. Sympathetic oversight must step in from time to time to help things go better than otherwise they would. We have to help the child think better and more patiently and more fruitfully than he could by himself. He grows only by what he does—but we can and must help.

Some people will ask, "Are we going to spoil the children if we act only indirectly?" To let this happen would be exactly the opposite of all that has here been said. Selfish whim is the very thing we are most opposed to, whether in children or in grown people. To become "more of a self" means to grow away from whims by taking always more and more into account. But it is the child who must take the more and more into account. He grows by what he does. If we try to help, it must be real help. Our danger is that we shall do the thinking and simply give the child the results of our thinking. There may be, and will be, times when we have to do this, but they should be the exceptions and not the rule. Otherwise, the child is deprived of the chance of becoming "more of a person." Happy the child whose parents can think together with him, really

think with him, hold their minds in suspense as together they and he make a real examination of the situation and conclude only in and through this examination.
In no other way, it appears, can parents help so well.

We may summarize the whole discussion by saying
that if the child is to become "more of a person," he
must act like a person, must act if possible like "more of
a person" than hitherto; and our part is to help him
thus to act up to his possibilities as a person—emotionally stable, thinking things through, accepting responsibility. The very young child cannot do this; he is not
yet a person in any full sense. But we must always have
in mind that he is to become a person and ever "more
of a person," and everything we do with him or for him
or around him must be judged as best we can in the light
of its bearings on him and his continued growth as a
person. In season and out I must help my child face
his situation with emotional stability, think things
through as best he can, and knowingly see and accept
responsibility.

Some perhaps will wonder that so little has been said
herein about school. The omission was intentional.
The traditional school, which most parents still think
of when they think school, was run on a plan that largely
disregarded and even opposed what is here advocated.
This older school is now being rapidly made over, and
we must all help in the process. It was largely for this
purpose that this article has been written. One principal
aim here has been to help parents think of a better education so that they will wish it for their children and demand it in their schools. In school or out, always and

everywhere, the chief thing—far and away more important than any subject-matter the school can teach—is that the child, the youth, and the man shall, with their fellows, ever be growing as persons. In education this must be our chief aim.

XV

THINKING IN CHILDHOOD AND YOUTH*

Ｈow shall we bring up a child in respect to his thinking, especially his thinking where religion is involved? This question, with its varied ethical and psychologic difficulties, is the problem before us. Shall I teach my child to think what I think? Have I the right so to do? If yes, what I think now or what I thought at his age? If no, should I then teach him *to* think rather than *what* to think? If yes to this, can I manage it? Can I have him from infancy do his own thinking? And in the end not lose? Such questions as these with all their partial "yes" and "no" answers, with all the weal and woe they hold at stake—such questions so considered make up the difficulty of the task facing us.

In an earlier day, when reliance on authority as such was more acceptable, our question would for most have been answered before it arose. In that day those in charge must on all important matters teach the young the conduct and views that had been "settled." On that basis everything thought of as education—and with it much not so named—was precisely what will here be called "training" and "indoctrination." Since these terms carry in common use varying implications they are placed in quotation marks throughout this paper to

---

* *Religious Education*, February, 1928.

indicate that they are used in a special sense correlative
of the authoritarian character of the educative process
involved: on the one hand, authoritative dictation; on
the other, "docile" (unquestioning) acceptance, both
in the hope that the matters so taught might remain
settled.

Of course only in special places if anywhere could
one find "one hundred per cent" acceptance of such
authoritarianism. But in comparison with the present
unsettled state of affairs in this country one can easily
find times and places and respects in which a fairly unquestioning deference to authority as such has held sway
with a like acceptance of its correlative type of authoritarian instruction. Whether as cause or as effect, both
deference to authority and authoritarian education ("indoctrination") appear to prevail in any civilization in
the degree that social change is there absent.

At the present time there is wide diversity of attitude
in this matter of "indoctrination." Possibly most still
cling to it, though in varying degrees. Both lingering
practice and in lesser degree asserted right and duty il-
lustrate it. "Who owns your child? The state? Do
not you?" These questions were asked during the
Oregon school controversy about compulsory attendance
in public schools. And the answer was given in a question counted to answer itself: "If you don't own your
own child, what in the wide world do you own?" Others
said, "The right of the parent to select the mental and
moral training of the child is fundamental and inalienable—the most primary right recognized by enlightened
countries." We need not take sides over the question

there at issue to see in these quotations an unquestioned assumption of child "ownership." Admittedly, so runs the implication, somebody "owns" the child in such manner as to carry with it the right to decide "his mental and moral training" and this seems regarded as the necessary correlative of childhood. What if any part the state should have in such ownership might be debated, but a just right to "ownership" somewhere resident in the older generation—that was not questioned.

It would be a hasty generalization to conclude that the thought content thus held proper for "indoctrination" is limited to the field of religion. Powerful organizations seem at bottom to rest their propaganda interest in our schools on an assumption (by them unquestioned) that all teaching, whether of history or otherwise, is necessarily "indoctrination." With those who think thus it naturally becomes a serious matter as to who shall control the "indoctrination" of our pupils and to what end. On this basis our schools would become pawns in the contests of factions, as children have long been pawns in contests over dogmas.

However, it is not easy to shift all at once from a hitherto unchallenged practice. Many who have rejected the extreme "ownership" and "indoctrination" position now find themselves troubled as they face the consequent changed approach to the moral and religious education of their children. If we do not "indoctrinate," so they reason, what hope have we that our children will believe certain things essential to a religious outlook? And without this religious outlook what basis have we for an adequate moral character? In the di-

lemma thus seemingly fixed, many parents face acutely
the problem here set for our consideration.

With this preliminary glance at the field let us now
come to closer grips with our problem: How shall we
bring up a child in respect to his thinking? The inquiry seems at the outset to divide itself into two parts,
the one ethical, the other psychological. The one: What
is right? What should we seek to do in this situation?
What is the ideal? The other: In the situation of con-
crete realities, how much of the ideal is feasible to be
attempted and how shall we go about it?

There need be no objection to considering these two
questions separately, even though, as is freely admitted,
the ethical and the feasible are but different aspects of
the same process. There is, however, more reason than
mere facility of treatment for considering them separately. Ideal and obligation, as nearly related as they
are, do not cover quite the same ground. The moral
obligation of any situation may be, and probably is,
properly limited to what is feasible in that situation;
but it does not follow that the long-run ideal is to be
limited to what is at present feasible. On the contrary,
in the matter of ideals one's reach of vision should exceed one's grasp, else no far-reaching program can be
attempted. Indeed, for best conduct at any time the
ideal must exceed the feasible. The call to us is to go
as far as we can. Except by trial we cannot tell how far
we can go. Our conception of the ideal then should
always sketch out more than we can at present see how
to attain. On no other basis do we get the best guidance
for conduct.

What, then, is the ethics of our situation? Can we agree on a foundation principle in this matter of youthful thinking? The word foundation is a difficult one and in this region provokes many opinions. This much perhaps most will accept: Whatever else be true, our treatment of the young must look to making them eventually able to think for themselves, as able and disposed to think for themselves as we can effect. Differences of application will of course arise. Some will wish to postpone the "eventually" to a late day; others will say, "Why not now?" We may differ also over differences of "native endowment." But with the general statement as made most who read it will agree. Any who do not so agree will probably find little else to their liking in this account. Can we now give this general statement a more specific content?

To think is the essential factor and element of the general statement. Moral life depends on it. When we say "think for themselves," strictly speaking—as another has pointed out—the phrase "for themselves" is superfluous and redundant. One cannot really think without thinking for himself. But, taken in its connection, the phrase calls attention to the factor of personal and individual responsibility in a social situation. So considered, thinking is essential to self-hood—about as essential to self-hood in any ideal sense as any element can well be. On such thinking practical (moral) responsibility rests, since through it alone can the person as such ascertain in any responsible fashion or degree the demands of any situation. Certainly thinking is necessary to intelligent and effectual moral action.

If such thinking is to be reliable and useful, it should, as far as possible, be based on a technique quite independent of the particular merits at issue and should proceed independently of prejudice. By the comparison and criticisms of actual instances of thinking it becomes possible to improve our technique of thinking, to locate and define prejudice in such a way as to help us to get loose from it, and thus in the end to get a clearer ideal of a type of thinking that shall be free from all such blemishes. This resulting ideal of unwarped thinking we wish especially to set up as an aim and effort in the matter before us. It is well to be reminded that the kind of thinking here considered is really an adventure into the unknown. Thinking that merely repeats past conclusions ceases to be thinking and becomes instead automatic conduct. Thinking in any full true sense is the process of finding the best way of meeting a novel situation. Any region not fully explored may afford opportunity for true thinking. And the result is always an adventure. The outcome cannot be foretold. Emerson well said, "Beware when God Almighty turns loose a thinker." In lesser degree but still in a true sense the warning holds of any instance of real thinking. It is exactly this uncertainty that troubles those whose greatest fear is for the fixedness of what is, for the safety of vested interests of any kind, whether of property or of propriety or of doctrine. If people are allowed to think "freely," there is in fact no telling what they may conclude. And the perturbation of those apprehensive produces a characteristic result. The less inherent security any situation has to offer for a vested interest, the more inclined are the interested ones to fear for the outcome and in their fear to search for authoritarian support and to shun an untrammeled and unbiased inquiry. And they are in their day and generation right. Thinking is a hazardous adventure. It cannot be trusted to see things only in old lights, still less in prejudiced lights. The only real safety then is in preferring truth to vested interest. We must stake all on free inquiry. Our reliance thus is on thinking and our hope is to make it so reliable that we may trust its new disclosures.

But this discussion of thinking does not settle our problem. Many will agree with all so far said, yet feel the essential difficulty untouched. If my cherished doctrine will not finally stand the test of criticism, these will say, then I invite your criticism and I agree in advance to follow the argument at any cost. I will have the truth whatever it be. But, they will go on to say, I shall not give up my position on any shallow examination, least of all am I willing, when so much is at stake, to trust my child *in his immaturity* to the alluring sophisms of plausible but shallow students of life. My love for my child compels me to protect him till he is in fact able to think for himself. When that time comes I shall turn him loose, as indeed I must, but with the hope that by then his character will in the main be settled and his mind strong enough to make his thinking and his consequent conduct both reliable and defensible. So says many an anxious parent.

With such feelings every parent must feel sympathy. Children are so docile, so trusting, so little able to detect fallacies, so easily led in argument to give weight according to personal love and trust, and there is in these matters so much at stake, that every parent will feel responsibility for a just protection. But what protection is just and how shall we contrive to secure it? These are matters not easily settled, certainly not by a sentimental preference for our hitherto cherished views which makes us oblivious to a higher duty both to truth and to our children. We accordingly must call a sharp halt to any sentiment which would, under the guise of child protection, give *carte blanche* to any parent or group of parents or any adult organization whatever to fasten in their young any cherished belief which they in their prejudice happen to think necessary.

So important are the matters here involved that we must examine them more closely. First of all, it is abundantly proved by history that early training efficiently directed can and does fasten so firmly in the young our doctrinal positions, social, economic, religious, racial, nationalistic, that thereafter under all ordinary circumstances the bias so produced remains for most an effectual warping throughout life. Only the exceptional cases rid themselves of such "socially inherited" biases. If any doubt this conclusion, it is only necessary to ask how many in this country are Democrats and Republicans in conformity with their early home and community environment, how many in their church connections have followed their parents, how many, whether within or without the church, still maintain the prejudiced attitudes of their parents toward opponent groups, how many southern whites differ, say, from the French in their attitude toward Negroes. A fair study of the different and opposed reactions provoked by such words as Jew, Negro, Nordic, Catholic, Ku Klux, Al Smith, Jeff Davis, will show the depth and pervasiveness of early biases. If more be needed to convince, study the arguments advanced in defense of these prejudices and note the opposed gullibility on the one hand and the unquestioning rejection on the other that such arguments respectively meet. The possibility and strength of "indoctrination" are abundantly proved.

In all of this, be it noted, success at "indoctrination" is no guarantee of validity of doctrine. Opposed sides of the same doctrine lend themselves to the process with seeming impartiality. "Indoctrination" in trinitarianism (among orthodox Christians) is thus offset by "indoctrination" in unitarianism (among Mohammedans). Nearer home, hereditary Republicans offset hereditary Democrats; hereditary Catholics can be matched by hereditary Protestants. Wherever we find opposed doctrinal positions following family lines and regional boundaries we may be fairly sure that it is "indoctrination" and not reasoned connection that (on one side, at least) has produced the effect. Indeed, the wide prevalence of these continuing family lines and group boundaries in doctrinal oppositions almost causes us to question whether anything but "indoctrination" can be the rule. In any event, it is abundantly proved that success at indoctrination is no guarantee of validity of doctrine.

We may summarize the discussion to this point by concluding (i) that it is possible to "train" and "indoctrinate" a child in some factional or sectarian position in such fashion and degree that under ordinary conditions when he is old he will not depart from it; (ii) that success in this is no guarantee of the correctness of the position; (iii) that from a study of history the parents' belief in their own rectitude is likewise no guarantee of correctness of position. But this is not all. Without necessity of argument we may further assert (iv) that parents and other elders have often managed to use the child as means to the end of upholding some faction or dogma dear to their hearts. We need not impugn motives. The fact remains unshaken. In the light of all this it is, then, finally submitted that intentionally so to "train" and "indoctrinate" is (v) to violate fundamentally that respect for the child's personality essential to ethics and is besides in probability (vi) to do the child a positive disservice as he faces a civilization changing as never before. The last two indictments we shall now examine.

Under whatever terms we may choose to describe the position, "respect for personality" seems about as close to a fundamental principle of ethics as study has been able to find. The essential dignity and worth of human individuality and our obligation to develop and respect it in each other—these assumptions practically underlie all modern discussion of ethics. Harnack expressed the same thought when he found the essence of Christianity in the idea of the "infinite worth of the human soul." Kant expressed the same idea in his "kingdom of ends" —that we should treat humanity always as an end and never as a means merely. The same was implied in what was said above about getting each child to the place where he can and will think for himself. We may say it a little more elaborately by asserting that ethics demands such respect for personality as means the continued development and expression of each to the fullest degree possible in reciprocal relation with others. An essential constituent of this is a self-direction that respects a like self-direction in others. Such growing of all together is the highest duty. The conception, moreover, tests all social doctrines and institutions. Those, like the Sabbath, were made for man and not man for them. Everything we uphold must meet the test that it make for the growing of all together. From all this, it seems clearly to follow that there is no higher obligation than so to educate a child that increasingly he can and will think for himself reliably and ethically. In particular, we must conclude that normally the child shall eventually arrive at the place where he can and will review what he has hitherto heard and believed, and will subject it to the most searching and unbiased analysis and testing of which he is capable. If, contrary to this, we by our teaching so "indoctrinate" a child that he either cannot or will not think thus freely for himself, then we have not really or effectually respected his personality. We have instead enslaved him in fact to us and to our way of thinking. If we have done so knowingly and intentionally, we have then in this respect and to this degree willfully used him as means and not as end. We have used him as means to the support and perpetuation of a doctrine or faction which we have valued above him, above the development of his free personality, and above the hope and opportunity that he may improve over our thinking. To trust to the personality we are helping to build and thus to prefer the outcome of his fresh examination to the insight we have hitherto had, requires great faith and deep conviction; but nothing short of this can claim to be proper respect for the personality for whose growth we as parents are so peculiarly responsible, or proper regard for the society in which he is to live and act. Intentionally to "indoctrinate" seems a clear violation of our deepest ethical insight.

But this general ethical consideration is not all. Times are changing. To build, then, a static outlook on any point may prove a hurt. Although changes have always been going on, the present seems unique in that change is not only much more rapid now than ever before but it promises to become still more rapid. This fact of unique change sets a new and unique task for education. In the remote past social change was so slow that it was thus easy to think of education as properly a handing down from father to son of the unchanging social inheritance. Under such conditions "indoctrination" was all but inevitable. The more surely and precisely youth got its lesson, the more surely and precisely could it be applied. But the outlook now is different. Youth faces a changing future—a future that is in many, many respects unknown. To learn, then, in a static and unadaptable fashion may mean inability to adjust to some very significant change. The results may be tragic. Ability to think for oneself is thus essential. Without it, intelligent adaptation to change is impossible.

The moral situation seems here to demand peculiar

consideration. The official guardians of society's morals
have hitherto quite frequently held a philosophy highly
antagonistic to the idea of change. They have accordingly been unwilling to recognize the need of adaptation in the matter of morals. But new situations have
been arising with new moral demands. The automobile,
for example, has introduced a host of demands that our
morality is slow in rising to meet. There is great danger
that moral outlook and habits too often adjusted to
mere surface details will lag hurtfully behind the changing social situation. The situation is made worse by
the further fact that the same guardians have quite
generally taught morals on a taboo basis, surrounding
the whole matter with mystery and fear. Where the
taboo system succeeds it tends to make difficult the shift
of a person from one type of community and moral
situation to another. On a taboo basis of morals, the
thinking necessary upon such a shift is at times almost
impossible. And, saddest of all, where the taboo system
fails it tends to break down altogether.

But this yet is not the whole story. Our youth increasingly refuses to accept authoritarian morals. To
the consternation of many, it demands the why of right
and wrong. In a former day it might suffice for the
parents to say, "The Bible says so," or "The church so
holds," or "It simply isn't so done in polite circles";
but that day has largely passed. For weal or woe, youth
asks why; and, if a satisfactory why be not forthcoming,
it tends to think there is no sufficient why. In any event,
it wishes to take affairs into its own hands. We are
forced thus to put morals on an intelligent and "why"

basis or run the risk that the rising generation will have
no morals at all.   The why must be so seen and so accepted that it can hold fast amid change.   Mere habits,
however good, will not suffice.   The reason why must be
enthroned.   No type of authoritarian morals finds sufficient acceptance to meet the need.   Difficult though it
be, it is perhaps especially in the realm of morals that
we cannot afford to fail in preparing our children to
think eventually for themselves.

From whatever way we view the ideal to be followed
in the management of children and youth, the conclusion seems the same.   "Indoctrination" is a fundamental
moral infringement and a dangerous moral practice.
We should do our best to teach our children really to
think.

With what may be called the "ideal" demands of the
situation thus definitely before us, let us now face the
"feasible."   At once many will agree that "in the end"
the child must think and decide for himself, but will
say that it is not feasible to put all his education from the
beginning on this basis and therefore that parents are
not only justified in teaching their children what they
themselves think, but compelled so to do.   "Indoctrination," these will conclude, is therefore inevitable.   There
is so much truth in this that some readers will be dis-
appointed in the conclusions about to be drawn.   What
are the facts as to procedure and what shall be done
about them?

At this point a more detailed definition of the term
"indoctrination" may prove helpful.   "Indoctrination"
necessarily implies implanting a position on some doc-

trine. The process in the bad sense used throughout this paper is opposed to education of the best kind both in the manner in which it is conducted and in the outcome likely to result. As regards manner, education becomes "indoctrination" in the degree that what is taught is taught on other than the merits of the case seen and accepted as such by the learner. As concerns result, education becomes "indoctrination" in the degree that the learner becomes thereby indisposed and unfit later to reconsider the question on its merits. As regards intent, in the degree that steps are taken to produce such an unquestioning outcome and attitude, in like degree may we say that the "indoctrination" is intentional.

Is "indoctrination" then inevitable? The answer in the judgment of this writer is mixed. It is both "yes" and "no": "yes" as to partial fact, but "no" as to intent. In some measure, "indoctrination" is inevitable, but license is not therefore granted. To some extent, "indoctrination" is the inevitable accompaniment of growing up in the particular environment. Do what you will to prevent it, much "indoctrination" will none the less ensue. Each specific environment will necessarily carry a certain amount of its peculiar "indoctrination." Does it, therefore, follow that parents are justified in conscious and intentional "indoctrination"? The answer is that it does *not* so follow. Because we cannot avert all of an evil it does not follow that we are therefore licensed to increase the evil. If "indoctrination," in spite of being an evil, proves very difficult of control, the greater reason for giving attention to the problem. What can be done and how shall we do it?

It requires but little consideration to see that the younger the child the less can we hope to put his learning, his acceptance of what he learns, on a basis of full and impartial consideration of the merits involved. He must build habits of regular eating and sleeping, to mention no more, before he can weigh the merits of these practices, months and even years before. We who are in control must meanwhile utilize the laws of habit formation to his good, so far as we can ascertain it. But this conclusion regarding the process of the child's early education in no way lessens the parental obligation to know all that is happening and to reduce "indoctrination" to the smallest feasible compass, and in particular to avert it as an abiding result. We shall, as early as we can and as much as we can, teach the "why" of all that is taught. When little brother pulls little sister's hair, he should, as soon as he can learn it, associate how little sister feels with his learning not to pull. We have to begin in bare parental control, but we do not have to stay there. Not all of the Golden Rule can be taught at once and we need not wait for full understanding before building habits of regard for others. The "what" in actual habit of conduct need not wait hurtfully for the "why." But at no time shall we so teach the "what" as to prevent the later fair consideration of the "why."

The general conclusion is easy. I shall teach the actual habits required in life as the need arises, taking care always that the accompanying attitudes are the best attainable. In connection, I shall teach as much of the "why" as I feasibly can. At the first this "why" part will be exactly nil. Beginning later, the "why" will from

then on receive more and more attention. When sufficient growth has been attained (but as early as feasible),
the "why" of the previously learned "what" will be
brought to the bar of attention. At all times the aim will
be the earliest and fullest measure of thinking com-
patible with other just demands of the situation. In
no instance shall we allow any doctrine to be enthroned
even approximately beyond recall, especially in the
matter of our own cherished beliefs. And we shall avoid
as much as we can commitment to doctrines on any
authoritarian basis, encouraging early efforts at sus-
pended judgment and often suggesting opposed positions to our own. Our consistent aim shall be not only
to avoid "indoctrination" but to build positively against
it.

Just here many will ask whether there are not some
things so well settled by experience that they can and
should be taught once and for all, and as fixedly as we
know how. It is impossible not to feel sympathetic
with this position if it be moderately held. Honesty,
truth-telling, courtesy, a Golden-Rule consideration for
others, for example, would seem sufficiently authenti-
cated to be taught with assurance. So much we may
grant, but there appears from it little or no justification
for "indoctrination." If experience has been obvious
enough to settle these matters for the race, the like experience will be available to help teach our children.
The beginnings of honesty may well be laid in authority,
but the "why" of it all is so obvious that from teaching
considerations we should wish to use it early in the
process. With increase of experience, the more subtle

aspects of honest dealings should receive attention; otherwise plausible dishonesties may go unrebuked. But all this is exactly to say that we are not to teach honesty on a mere "indoctrination" basis. Something much better is both possible and necessary. The rub will come when some will wish to include among the "settled" matters doctrines that are still controversial. This is to be expected, but no less to be resisted. The itch to "indoctrinate" assumes many disguises.

Certain difficult cases deserve special consideration here. What, if anything, shall I teach about God? What shall I do with the Bible? What shall I do about authority in morals?

The matter of authority in morals probably gets its importance in this connection from an assumed theory that all learning normally takes place only as the learner accepts the thing to be learned on the dictum of someone else taken as authority. It need hardly be said that such a conception of how learning takes place finds little acceptance with students of the subject. It is quite true that the authority of teacher or parent may bring about the practice necessary to fix some matter of learning. But, if so, it is the practice, not the authority, that brings about the learning. It is further true that the word of the teacher or of other authority may give some item of learning such standing and acceptance that it will accordingly become in time well fixed in the learner's mind or character. But, if so, it was the actual acceptance (along with practice) that did the fixing. The word of authority as such is not necessary to such acceptance. On the contrary, personal experience gives as a rule bet-

ter and more wholesome acceptance and in so far brings
quicker and sounder (more moral) learning than does
the "say so" of any one else. Certain older theories of
ethics did found the basis of right and wrong in the
authoritative will of God, and many seem to think that
all morals must be so taught, but so far as appears this
position is now seldom or never upheld in our better
institutions of learning. We conclude that the practical
authority of parents and teachers may play a proper part
in the moral nurture of the young, but that this is a very
different thing from enthroning authoritarianism in the
very heart of the learning process. Morals are to be
learned in the same ways as are other things.

What to teach about God and the Bible turns partly
on the question of authoritarian morals. That early
morals can and often should be put for the time on
an authoritarian basis may well be admitted, but what
about older children? There was a time in the not remote past when youth accepted authority in morals, at
least intellectually, but, as has already been said, that
day seems past. The general spirit of questioning has
descended from scientists to adults in general and thence
in turn to young people. With the general spirit of
inquiry abroad in the world it seems the height of unwisdom to attempt to found the morals of our children
on a basis that will not stand the test of inquiry whether
this be the authority either of God or of the Bible. The
old doctrine of plenary inspiration is now thoroughly
discredited, as likewise are the older anthropomorphic
conceptions of Deity, so that any building on them is
positively hazardous. So probably will such a founda-

tion later crumble that it is difficult to see how any intelligent and informed parent will be willing to risk
his child's future to such a procedure.

Apart from authority in morals what shall we teach
about God and the Bible? So far as this writer can see,
the general considerations urged in this paper apply here
as elsewhere. We should not only avoid "indoctrination"; we should build positively against it. But some
special dangers need to be considered if any reverence
for religion is to survive on a defensible basis. First of
all, we should deal fairly with our children as to the
authority of the Bible. Some seem to think they may
with impunity teach outworn theories to the young
in the hope that they will safely outgrow them. To do
so is to risk the confidence of our children in us and in
our essential rectitude. We cannot afford such risk.
The inherent psychology of the Bible is extraordinarily
true, but much of its history and most of its science are
not true. We must be truthful to our children. Similarly with the miracles of the Bible, it would seem much
better to tell our children from the first that people used
to believe such things but we now do not.

What to teach about God is perhaps the most difficult
question of all. There is such wide diversity as to what
is finally true that we may expect any specific position
we teach later to be questioned, and the more dogmatic
the position the more surely will it be questioned and
the more likely will it be rejected. We certainly run a
very great risk if we teach a God whose moral standards
are lower than those now commonly accepted among
men. We cannot, then, in wisdom teach the god of

orthodoxy. The risk is too great. Whatever we do
teach we should teach with due regard to the uncertainty
involved. Not to do so would seem an immoral pro-
ceeding.

What about teaching religion? If possible this is even
more difficult to answer than about God. It is a rash
prophet who says that man will eventually reject religion. History, so far as I can read it, is against such a
prophecy. We do, however, seem not rash but wise to
expect that religion will increasingly base itself, in the
words of Sabatier, not on the authority either of book
or of church but of the "spirit," the way it works when
we try it. If so, it behooves all who believe in "spiritual"
values to found them on this rock of experience and not
on the sands of tradition, however hallowed this may be
by association.

To trifle with the welfare of our children is the thing
furthest from our wishes. The condition that faces us
is serious. We dare not gamble away either our children's confidence in us or their interest in the "spiritual" values of life. We surely do both if we teach
them as true what they later must dismiss as false.
It may be—who knows to the contrary?—that the truest
and most helpful thing we can finally teach our children is our own uncertainty with our deepest insight as
to what is at stake—these along with the best methods
of attack the world has yet devised. If we do this
we have at least been honest with them and with
ourselves. Honest doubt, sincere yearnings, method of
attack—these three have worked wonders in science;
why not here?

XVI

INTELLIGENCE, INDIVIDUAL DIFFERENCES, AND DEMOCRACY

FROM time to time we hear it asked whether human intelligence as actually distributed will suffice to make a success of democracy. It is of course clear that men differ in intelligence, and these varying abilities seem distributed according to the uniform curve. Such a distribution means that, though there are few idiots, there are correspondingly few geniuses; and therefore that most people fall in between, with the greatest number toward the middle. The question thus arises regarding democracy, where policies are decided by majority vote, as to what chance wisdom has to rule? Ought we not under such circumstances, it is asked, give up democracy and seek instead some form of government that will insure the rule of the wise over the many?

In partial answer, at least two important principles can be stated.

1. Lesser intelligence can appropriate, and use intelligently, what only superior intelligence can invent or devise. For example, the large majority can now learn enough of the germ theory to guard reasonably against known infection, although it took thousands of years of study culminating in such a genius as Pasteur to prove that germs carry disease. More specifically,

just ordinary law-makers and enforcers can now drain
swamps and kill mosquitoes, even though the problem
of malaria and yellow fever had baffled the world's greatest minds throughout the whole of history up to a bare
generation ago. Granted that only the few will perform
the great acts of discovery and invention, it is just as true
that the many can afterwards learn to use intelligently
the results of these great discoveries and inventions. It
is in this way (as we shall see in a moment) that the mass
of people may hope to build the intelligence needed for
coping with difficult social problems.

What has just been said need not mean (and does not,
for this writer) that we are to set aside in advance certain
ones as the most gifted and look exclusively to them
to discover for the rest of us. This would probably be
both unwise and unjust. We literally do not know how
to pick those who will in fact so lead. Leadership is of
many kinds and depends on many factors. Moreover,
almost everyone leads at some time and follows at other
times. And actual leadership emerges out of the situation. And, still further, the followers at any time have
to be intelligent if they are to co-operate wisely. These
considerations lead now to the second important principle.

2. Intelligence can be built. This is an assertion that
some will at first doubt, the common discussion of in-
telligence-testing having served to confuse them. These
think of intelligence as simply and solely innate. This
is as great a mistake as to say that the base of a rectangle
suffices, without reference to the altitude, to determine
the area. Actual working intelligence always involves

both "nurture" and "nature." Geometry teaches us that rectangles having equal altitudes differ from each other according to their bases, and also just as truly that rectangles having equal bases differ from each other according to their altitudes. In much the same way we can say as regards power to deal with any given situation, that men of equal native ability will differ from each other according to their varying nurtures (or opportunity at learning along the line under consideration); and similarly that men of equal nurture (or opportunity along that line) will differ from each other according to their varying native abilities.

It is on this last proposition as a basis that intelligence tests are built. Their makers seek such common and everyday questions and items as that all to be tested have had equality of opportunity to learn them, so that the differences in ability to answer the questions may truly indicate differences in native ability. Where the tests have been standardized in a given population homogeneous as regards cultural opportunity (say among well-to-do urban old-stock American whites), they seem as applied within that population to prove increasingly reliable indices of comparative native ability. But where tests standardized as stated are applied to sufficiently different populations (say to rural mountain whites or to the children of Sicilian immigrants or to southern rural Negroes), the comparative results are not reliable. These groups have not had an equal opportunity with the original population to learn the subject matter of the tests. They may be just as natively capable, but the tests will not show it.

What has just been said implies that each specific culture builds its own type of intelligence, and this is true. But it is also true, and susceptible, it appears, of historic demonstration (as we see below), that a group culture can itself be so built as to increase the actual intelligence of its aggregate group members. This proposition is so important that we must examine it carefully.

Probably there is no better single measure (or definition) of intelligence than the comparative ability to sense and solve a difficult novel problem. If two persons face a given situation and one of them senses and solves a crucial problem involved in the situation, while the other either does not sense the problem or, seeing it, cannot solve it, then we say that the first man acted more intelligently or showed more intelligence as regards that situation. In this matter of culture and intelligence we may profitably contrast the Stone Age with the present state of Western civilization. It is generally accepted in this field of study that children are born now little if any more able than then. If, therefore, we can show that adults now manifest more ability at sensing and solving problems than then, we should have indication of an actual increase in effectual intelligence from then to now. Boaz tells us (*Anthropology and Modern Life*, 1932 ed., p. 132) that in the Stone Age mankind went for 30,000 years without improving upon his stone implements. When we contrast this long period of no significant invention in this area with the number of significant inventions continually being made among us, especially in the past century or so, we are forced to admit that something has happened. Let us try to state more precisely what it is that has thus happened.

Imagine the people of the Stone Age distributed on a scale of intelligence (i.e., of ability to sense and solve novel problems). We need not doubt that they had invented their stone implements or that they did solve some novel problems. But making new inventions along the line of useful physical implements, this was a problem beyond even their greatest geniuses for 30,000 years. On their scale of intelligence this problem lay, during that whole period, somewhere outside and beyond their highest reach. But since their day man has introduced a more rapid rate of invention. In fact, within the past four hundred years we have discovered how consciously to discover. So that now we sense and solve ever-new problems at an ever more rapid rate, specifically at a rate vastly superior to that of the Stone Age. In this true and verifiable sense mankind has extended his actual working intelligence (as compounded of nature and nurture) up the scale far beyond the highest reach of the Stone Age. And it is not only the geniuses now that surpass the former highest; many, many people of lesser abilities in our day make new inventions. It cannot be denied that mankind has thus built to much higher levels than was true in the Stone Age his effectual intelligence along the lines indicated by scientific discovery and invention.

As we study this marvelous achievement, we see that it is made possible by the fact of culture, the social heritage of cumulative human achievement, and its significant improvement. At first very, very slowly, then more rapidly, has the culture grown: along the lines of noticing differences in the cultures of different groups, of asking and answering questions about these differences, of discussing ideas as such, of studying and criticizing ideas, of expecting (after the death of Socrates) that at least a few would criticize the common stock of ideas with reference to improving them. Later, at long length, came the suggestion of consciously testing ideas by the way they work out when tried. Since that advance the process of discovery and invention has been greatly accelerated.

Moreover, general growth has come from the fact that each such advance has, in proportion to apparent significance and to ease of acquisition, been built, at least eventually, into the common culture, there to be given within varying limits to all born within the group. So that at length our Western culture has ceased to be static in effect and instead has become dynamic, taking on now the characteristic of consciously expecting and seeking improvements. That the first great modern advance came in the physical realm need not surprise us. It has meanwhile extended itself mightily to some phases of the biological (as for example, the germ theory of disease mentioned earlier), and now belatedly enters the psychologic and social areas. Culture is in essence communicable intelligence: it grows continually upon its own growth.

When we compare the human ability distribution curve as it now is with what it was in the Stone Age, we see that the low end remains now (so far as we can tell) just where it then was. Our idiots (except such as medicine or surgery can reach) are born and remain no higher than theirs. Our children (we believe) are born at about the same level as were theirs. But our curve of effectual intelligence has along many and perhaps most lines extended itself at the upper reaches far beyond anything they knew or could conceive. We have (probably) a uniform distribution curve, but so probably had they. And it is not only the highest of the population that have advanced. If the curve remains (as we believe) uniform in shape, this must mean that the central (mediocre) region also has moved up the line. The common man can actually think better (sense and solve many harder problems) than formerly he could.

This argument from historic anthropology that working intelligence is a product of the effectual culture finds corroboration from the current psychological researches into the "problem of heredity and environment." Identical twins, admittedly equal at the start, subjected to widely differing cultural environments, have shown differences in I. Q. of as much as twenty-four points. The pertinent evidence seems conclusive that the kind of intelligence measured by the intelligence tests may, and perhaps generally does, improve when the environment is culturally improved.

How the better culture thus improves the intelligence is but the repetition of what was said earlier. The culturally better home uses finer distinctions of meaning and adheres to them more consistently. The children in such a home acquire and use these finer dis-

tinctions and build interests upon them that in turn
call for still finer distinctions. The human mind is not
a muscle nor a faculty, but an organized aggregate of
meanings functioning in life. These meanings have all
been learned, largely in the self-other relationship, and
at least all the beginning ones largely from the culture.
Whatever, then, intellectually up-builds the culture up-
builds in turn the mind or intelligence using that culture.

In all of this discussion it has been constantly implied
that the effectual intelligence at any time under discussion lies of course along its own peculiar line. We
have built intelligence especially in the realm of natural
science and, to a lesser degree, in various biological regions. But up to now the social sciences lag. This, we
may believe, is partly because this region is more complex and therefore more difficult, but also partly because
intelligence has here not been given so free a rein. Especially has freedom to experiment been discouraged,
apparently because the mighty have feared lest experiment would question the right of their might. But
under existing conditions our greatest problems and
most serious evils lie exactly in the social-economic-
political area. We dare not shut our eyes to the evils,
nor our minds to the problems. That we do not now
know the answers to the problems in this area need no
longer deter us. What man has done, man can do. We
must set out consciously to build within our people the
needed social intelligence for coping with these urgent
social problems.

And this seems the answer to the question about de-

mocracy. We must not give it up if by any means it can
be made to work. Mankind has tried despotism, whether
of one or of the few, and always it grows selfish, even
where it does not so begin. If anything has been histor-
ically proved, it is that autocracy does not in the long
run succeed. The record of democracy is better. So
that, as we face our present difficulties, democracy can
still probably be made to work. If education can be
directed to the building of intelligence (and it can),
democracy can face the future with courage, even though
not with certainty. Granted time and the proper effort,
the needed intelligence can probably be built.

To the group, then, nature sets no barriers, only to
individuals. There are no limits to the aggregate social
intelligence that can be built. It is in this way that we
can grapple with our serious social problems. Granted
time and the proper effort, we may believe that what is
needed to be done can be done.

XVII

BUILDING SOCIAL
INTELLIGENCE*

MODERN social change differs so greatly in degree from anything that preceded it that it is in effect different also in kind. The key to this new kind of change is modern experimental science. Before the time of Galileo, if intelligent men differed in opinion, they either appealed to recognized authority or started from accepted principles and argued the matter out. But when Galileo dropped the balls from the leaning tower of Pisa he inaugurated a new era in logic: the testing of opinion by experiment. Out of this new principle have come conscious and controllable discovery and the consequent accumulation of tested and reliable results: the immediate twofold cause of the growth of modern natural science and the ultimate cause of modern social change.

Before modern science arose, theology taught, and men generally believed, that man's natural and unaided reason was unreliable. But with the coming of science and the accumulation of tested knowledge men gradually forgot the curse of Adam and achieved a new faith in human intelligence. In the exercise of this new faith, they have subjected the whole of traditional culture to critical scrutiny; partly to determine what henceforth to believe; partly—and this especially concerns us—

* *Journal of Adult Education,* April, 1936.

to change the traditional culture into forms that will better serve men's needs. The conscious control of social life through the conscious remaking of culture is the great problem of our own time, though many among us still hold back through fear of men's inability to control their own cultural development.

Even more obvious and possibly more powerful than man's new faith in his own intelligence is another effect produced by science. This is the application of scientific principles to all fields of human endeavor and concern: industry, transportation, communication, agriculture, medicine, to name only a few. It seems fair to say that, as scientific discoveries are increasing in geometric ratio, so also are inventions and the consequent changes in human living.

Thus, change is the great new factor in history. Older philosophies taught that change in fundamentals was impossible and that in ordinary affairs it was accidental, trivial, and bad. Now no philosophy adequate to deal with life as it is can fail to accord to change a fundamental place in its system. Formerly, social stability was sought by forbidding and preventing change; now such a course would be social suicide. To try to stop change is to try to dam up irresistible pressures. We want change, but we want it to be orderly. To direct change intelligently is the supreme task of our civilization.

Any group culture to be adequate must form one consistent working whole, in which ways of producing, ways of distributing, ways of living, ways of governing, ways of ordering conduct fit suitably together and support one another. Such an effective balance is likely to be

achieved in a culture where conditions of life remain
stable for a long time. But in a culture like ours, where
science and technology are continually bringing changes,
institutional forms are likely to get out of date and lag
behind. Social stresses thus arise. These must be re-
lieved by changing the lagging parts and bringing them
abreast of the more forward developments. Perpetual
intelligent criticism with continual intelligent change
of institutions is the price that a civilization growing
rapidly along any one line must pay for that growth.

When we have accepted the inevitability and desira-
bility of social change, how are we to decide what changes
are needed and how we can bring them about? We
are offered a variety of radically opposed answers to these
questions. In this country one very common answer is
a denial of the need for serious change. We have prospered in the past; we shall prosper again, runs the
argument. We prospered, so those who hold this view
continue, because government did not interfere with business; when business is once more given a free hand,
prosperity will return. This argument cannot be answered in detail here, but one big new fact that has
changed conditions for most people in this country may
be pointed out.

In 1860, Abraham Lincoln said that any poor but
healthy man might "look forward and hope to be a hired
man for this year and the next, work for himself afterwards, and finally to hire men to work for him." When
farming was the main occupation and cheap land in
the West was virtually limitless, there was no reason

why Lincoln's formula should not work. But now, when most men no longer work on farms and when frontier lands are no longer available, men hire themselves out not for two years but for life, or rather for so long as business conditions are good. Business conditions thus become the determining factor. Independence has given way to dependence. And with this fundamental change further changes become imperative.

The dictators of Europe and of Asia are giving the most striking answer to the problem of controlling social change, but this is an answer diametrically opposed to that of democracy. Under a dictatorship, power is seized by one man, or by a few men, self-chosen. The dictator takes charge of all agencies of public opinion—the press, the radio, libraries, universities, schools—in order that his control may be absolute. Thoughts, opinions, even facts themselves are supplied by the government and manipulated to suit the dictator's purposes. Contrast this situation with a democracy, where the social changes needed to bring the various elements in the cultural whole into proper working balance are voted by the people as they see the need and because they see the need.

There are in our own country today many who tend toward accepting the attitude of a dictatorship: a distrust of the people's ability to think out weighty and difficult problems. And all of us must admit that, in the midst of propaganda put forth by narrowly selfish and powerful interests, wise decisions are very difficult and, on any short view, uncertain. The whole situation is made more discouraging by certain psychologists, who pointedly teach that only comparatively few persons can think. So democracy stands discounted in its own house. And, among the critics of democracy, two groups openly assert that dictatorship is the only way out: one advocating a dictatorship of those who in the past have largely controlled our society and still control it; the other advocating a dictatorship of the proletariat.

No such pessimistic view of democracy as that indicated above is necessary; certainly, not yet. There are available resources that have not been tried. Some of the most important of them have been hidden by a misconception of the nature of intelligence, fostered by certain psychologists. With that misconception cleared, the building of intelligence adequate to effectual democracy becomes not only a possibility but a very promising probability.

Following the line of thought in the preceding chapter, let us re-examine the nature of intelligence and consider the possibility of building higher levels of social intelligence. It is admitted even by the psychologists in the opposition that a person's effective ability in regard to any difficult line of inquiry or conduct depends upon two factors: his native ability and his working knowledge of the situation involved. For instance, it is clear that any chemical engineer of today, even though he have only ordinary native ability, can, if he will work at his problem long enough, learn to direct manufacturing operations that would have been utterly impossible to even the greatest geniuses of a century ago. Through the researches of the great masters there has been accumulated a store of chemical knowledge that can be put at the disposal of lesser minds. And thus effectual intelligence in chemistry has been built to a higher level. What is true of chemistry is true also of every field of knowledge or endeavor in which modern science has made great improvements. And, when we remember that one of the contributions of science is a method of research by which conscious and controllable discovery is made possible, we can confidently assert that man has within the last three hundred and fifty years greatly increased effectual human intelligence in the realm of natural science. The record proves it. He who runs may read.

Now what man has done man can do. What he has done in chemistry has in some measure already been done also in agriculture, in medicine, and in other biological sciences. There appears no sufficient reason why it may not be done in the realm of the social sciences. To accomplish the desired end of building adequate social intelligence will undoubtedly take time, for ignorance and selfishness both stand as definite blocks in the way of social experimentation and of criticism of such experimentation. But there is no reason to believe that anything like three hundred and fifty years will be required. There are already in existence too many promising beginnings.

The place of conscious education in a program of democratic social change has by now been fairly well indicated. Its function is to build social intelligence along the lines of our social problems. There are two sides to such building. One is primarily the devising and contriving of new proposals; the other is the sort of criticism of these proposals that renders the critics themselves effectually intelligent in regard to the things proposed. The actual devising of new proposals will probably be largely the work of the more gifted; but in a democracy the criticism must be common to the body of citizens, even though here also the more capable will lead the way.

However, since the mass of people must make choices, they must learn to make them intelligently.

But the building of social intelligence is, for every individual, a lifelong undertaking. The home should contribute as much as it can before the child goes to school, and the conscious development of social intelligence should be a part—possibly the core—of the educational program from the child's first day in school until he is too old to participate in civic affairs.

Provision for such education would seem to be three-fold: partly a matter of concerted creative study by the universities, partly the spread of such results through a greatly extended system of adult education, partly a bringing up of youth on the basis of the new discoveries and inventions.

The universities in their graduate schools, working, to be sure, with capable students and scholars everywhere, must by concerted effort study our social-economic-political situation as never before. New ideas must be sought; old and new ideas must be subjected to searching criticism; social experimentation must be encouraged and studied with every care. Our reliance here for

advance is on the proper working of intelligence itself.
Honest co-operative thinking begets new suggestions;
careful criticism sifts; experimentation tests. Progress
in thinking becomes thus probable.

We live in a democracy. The people must decide. We
must, then, extend the best kind of adult education to
the point where the whole population is seriously studying what social policies to adopt. That our universities
and this adult study must both be free to suggest and
study wherever thought may lead is but to repeat in
different words what is here being advocated. The
people must act, but they should act, must so act if we
are really to advance, upon the best available ideas to be
got from any source. A very great danger in modern
days is partisan propaganda. This new and wider adult
education must help people guard themselves against
any form of demagogic propaganda. It is genuine study
that is needed.

The lower schools—elementary, secondary, and arts
college—have their definite part to play in this building
of social intelligence. Most schools now, it seems fair
to assert, indoctrinate in certain obsolescent if not obso-
lete ideas. Uncritical patriotism is a common product.
Our pupils are led to believe that we have the most per-
fect government ever known on earth; that our country
has always been right; that, although the forces of sin
mostly win out in the present, as soon as history begins
to be written virtue and wisdom always prevail; that
our Constitution, with its checks and balances, its tri-
partite division of powers, and the Supreme Court in
particular—all these represent the acme of social intelli-

gence. To question any of these things is to sin against the social Holy Ghost. Along with all this goes also an indoctrination in rugged individualism and the worship of money success.

Perhaps, as the joint product of all the foregoing, we find the all-too-common antagonism in the American mind to cultural and intellectual excellence. The public scorn of the "highbrow," the ridicule of the "Brain Trust," the disparaging use of the academic cap and gown in cartoons—all this has its roots in the failure of the schools to build real respect for intelligence and excellence. It is, of course, true that the Hearst newspapers, the *Chicago Tribune,* and the like exploit this underlying distrust and antagonism to their selfish ends. But the cartoons wouldn't seem funny if the traditional schools had not first laid the foundation for them.

The social intelligence we seek must be a kind that does in fact deal with the social situation. Our young people—and the older ones of us too, for that matter— need to learn what the actual world of affairs is like today, what kind of world our modern science has given us, how it differs from the world of even a generation or so ago, what problems of reconstruction therefore face us. In order to learn these things they will have to study actual current controversial issues. It is with live-issue unsolved problems that citizens have to deal. Young people must therefore begin early to study such live-issue unsolved problems. To study solved problems—dead issues—is no adequate preparation for dealing with live problems; the technique of study is too different. And we dare not wait to begin this study until youth reach the days of their maturity. By that time the cares of this world and the deceitfulness of riches, if the youth are successful in business, will have taken possession of their souls. If they are not successful, the danger is reversed. We dare not trust either. Still further, as a never finished problem, young and old alike must learn to recognize and see through the efforts of partisan propaganda to lead us to its prior-chosen selfish conclusions. In all these practical ways must our schools build effective social intelligence.

The social intelligence to be built is not to be identified with any form of indoctrination or indeed with mere spread of social knowledge. Knowledge is, to be sure, an indispensable part of intelligence, but it does not of itself suffice to constitute intelligence. The new education must be one in which the pupils and students really live—live up to the best they can know and think. If we are to build social intelligence in the rising generation, they must, then, live social intelligence. And this means that the school must reach out and become identified in many ways with the community, so that young and old literally study and solve community problems together. When this is done, the highest ideas evolved in graduate study will become the common treasure-house to which adult citizens and the younger citizens-now-growing will together repair for suggestions in solving community problems. When all of these agencies thus work together at the common task of building a better world, a higher social intelligence is increasingly built. It is no easy matter, but it is feasible.

Part III

Toward a Philosophy
of Education

XVIII
SOME UNDERLYING
PRINCIPLES *

EFFORT will be made in this chapter to state some of
the more strategic principles underlying a philosophy
of education suitable to a democratic society. The principles here stated separately must not, however, be understood as existing and acting independently of each
other. On the contrary, the several principles not only
apply simultaneously to any one situation, but they mutually explain and support each other.

If any ask as to the justification of the principles
proposed, the answer is, first, that they represent generalizations drawn inductively from many centuries of
criticized experience. Through many centuries men
have been drawing generalizations and criticizing the
generalizations already previously formed. I am giving
you my choice from the world's generalizations. Sec-

---

* An address delivered in San Francisco in 1938.

ondly, I would say regarding them that they are here offered as hypotheses, hypotheses already, in my own opinion, in good part supported by actual experience, but still hypotheses to be experimentally tested further and accepted only upon further testing, by actual trial in the social process. I propose now seven principles. Nine are involved in all, but two have been elaborated earlier. (See Chapters VI and IX.)

1. *Life itself is a positive good—a good that is to be defined and approved in terms of itself, not something to be denied or reduced or simply to be postponed.*

In the history of mankind, there have been advocated many philosophies opposed to what I have just stated. Most of these are now obsolescent. They have viewed life differently. There have been various religions the world over that have seen life as an evil or at best as a transition to some later good state. The early Christians included many who looked out upon life in this ascetic fashion. Hindu theology taught the error and pain of individual living, and the ultimate desirable absorption of the individual into the unconscious world spirit. The immediate spiritual ancestors of many of us sang these words,

"This world is a wilderness of woe.
This world is not my home."

They also sang,

"I'm a pilgrim, and I'm a stranger.
I can tarry, I can tarry but a night."

Now, in opposition to all of this, I am proposing first,

to think of the good life as good exactly in terms of life itself. The good life is a life good to live, just as music is good to hear or a landscape is good to see. Not that all life is good—far from it; but that we learn by actually living those kinds of life that are good or at any rate better than other kinds. We learn by criticizing the different kinds of life and by actual trial. From this point of view, the moral good is a service function to the life good to live. It makes life better—better to live. I am proposing accordingly, that the basis of ethics is human wants. A good is the recognized answer to a want. Wants, however, get in each other's way. Goods conflict. We have to choose. Whenever we begin to think about such matters, we have already a set of values on hand, criticized goods that we live by already more or less closely. We start, then, with that set of values and learn to criticize them in order that we may improve upon them. Many acts of conduct affect the happiness, that is, the good life of other people. Man accordingly learned long ago to hold each human individual responsible for what he thus does to affect others, to hold him responsible for the foreseeable consequences of his acts. The correlative obligation to this we call a moral obligation. We demand this moral obligation of all men.

It follows from the foregoing that all institutions, all types of conduct, all standards of living, and all human rights, are to be judged by their tendency to bring the good life to all concerned. You read in the Declaration of Independence of certain "inalienable rights." The better-thinking man has gone beyond

that now. From what I have just said, there can be no
such thing as inalienable rights; for any proposed right
must be judged by the way it works out when tried, the
way it works in bringing the good life to all affected.
If any right thus claiming to be inalienable were in fact
inalienable, we could not profitably criticize it. If it
did not work well, we could not change it. So we now
say that all rights are held subject to the way they affect
the good life of all concerned.

So much for the first principle. Various parts and
aspects of it will be made clearer as the other principles
are discussed.

2. *Personality as such is to be cherished in all men,
and, as far as possible, cherished on terms of equality.
The moral obligation to this is universal.*

This principle repeats in part what has just been said
in the first principle but from a different angle. Personality is the individual structural side of life. Only
individual persons live. There is no humanity over
and above the individual persons. To cherish and respect personality means to seek for each human individual, on equal terms with all others, the fullest feasible
good life possible to him. This means to develop and
express all—each one along with the rest—to develop
and express each one as far as feasible, and again on
terms of equality.

Now, as we think of developing anyone, education is
the very essence of the developing process. Education is
therefore essential to this second principle. Morality
can be again defined in terms of this principle. Some
acts, as I have said before, perhaps all acts, affect the lives

of others for good or ill. Most people learn, at least in the more usual personal affairs, to act upon this fact that what they do affects others. Thus, most people do in this way respect the personality of others more or less. The culture stores up distinctions and modes of appropriate conduct for treating others properly. These distinctions and modes of conduct we call morals and manners. Manners in this sense are but lesser morals. The culture, as I have said, stores up these distinctions and teaches observation of them to succeeding generations.

Now, these things that I have just said are facts known in history; and they show that obedience to moral obligations is a further social fact already well existing. There is, then, no point in asking (as some have proposed) whether the laws of nature allow freedom of moral action. If I may speak philosophically, it is an instance of *solvitur ambulando:* the question is solved in the practicing of it. The actual facts of considerable moral conduct on the part of most people are matters of everyday life known and observed of all men. Any theoretical question as to the possibility of morality simply does not exist. The practical questions are: first, as to whether we can make yet finer and better distinctions than those hitherto made in this field, and, secondly, a still more practical question, How can we bring it about that the best already known shall be well observed? In other words, the problem of morals is practical and not theoretical.

So much for the first two principles, that life is good, and that we owe universal obligations to respect the personality of each one. Those two go together to reinforce each other.

We come now to a third principle: that of change. One hundred years ago, no one in the world could have discussed change as I am going to discuss it now.

3. *Change is inherent in human affairs.* (This they would have agreed to.) *The future is not yet fixed.* (This they would not have agreed to.) *Effort counts, but the event is precarious. Our logic must accordingly shift from its former static basis to a dynamic basis.*

This principle intends to assert that the stream of human affairs develops continually in novel fashion. Neither history nor life, individual life nor life as a whole, ever repeats itself exactly. Each succeeding stage builds itself upon the preceding accumulation. If this be true (and it is true), each event is thus always novel. Moreover, it is (as we shall see in a moment) uncertain and precarious. We never know just what will happen, and that makes all the difference in behavior.

I said just above that this discussion could not have been given one hundred years ago. I am, however, only calling attention to life as we all know it today. The older views, however, were different. Various ancients believed in what they called fate. They believed that certain important events were fixed in advance to come to pass irrespective of what intervened, irrespective of what happened in between. If you read the old literature, you find that those who believed in fate believed that somehow the thing that was to be shaped the things that preceded it so that it could be. We don't now believe it possible that what is to be can shape the thing

preceding it. We believe that the things preceding shape
things that happen afterwards. The ancients, I have
said, believed in fate. Later there was a strong agreement between various theologians and the scientists that
the whole future down to the last detail had been fixed
once and for all in advance. As Omar Khayyam put it,

"Yea, the first morning of creation wrote
    What the last dawn of reckoning shall read."

The theologians and the scientists agreed with this
theory. One group said that events were fixed according to the will of God or the foreknowledge of God.
The other said they were fixed by the universal reign of
law. In either instance the results were the same for
present purposes: namely, that all future events are
already now fixed. If that were true, then forethought
and effort could not be what they seem. The position
here taken is in opposition: namely, that forethought
and effort are what they seem. The future is not yet
fixed. Human effort does, within limits, count. Human effort does, within limitations, fix what is going to
happen. Man thinks and acts more or less creatively
and his efforts actually help to determine what will
happen.

Each change that takes place grows in part out of the
past; but in an infinite universe chance is a real factor
to determine how things will come together. Each event,
then, is more or less uncertain, not entirely fixed by the
past; for this element of chance enters. The outcome is
always precarious. We never know precisely what will
happen. Always, then, the new and unexpected appear

co-mingled with the old and familiar. We strive to control what is happening and make it happen our way, and in this control the old and the familiar give us whatever basis we have for hope and effort; but the outcome is precarious. We never know just what will come. The universe is thus, as William James put it, open towards the future. The lid is off. Geology and evolution taught men thus to think, and this view calls for a dynamic logic in place of the older static logic.

Plato and Aristotle started men to thinking along the older lines. Mathematics was the basis of their thinking more than anything else. Up to the time of Descartes, mathematics reflected this static logic. Descartes introduced analytical geometry. Newton and Leibniz followed with the calculus, which is the mathematics of the ratio of change and how it takes place. Until about a century ago, however, men still thought that Euclidian geometry was absolutely true. Beginning in 1823, mathematicians began to understand that our ordinary geometry may not be true. There arose, then, three geometries, one just as logical as the other; and no mathematician who knows what he is about will tell you that either one is known to be true. Nobody knows which of either of these or of still other geometries is true. Quite recently Einstein has questioned (and there are some facts to corroborate his doubt) that Euclidian geometry is true among the stars. I mention this because it was the Euclidian geometry that especially formed the basis of the old logic.

We are discussing change. It was the eighteenth century that first conceived the idea of progress. Before that time men had thought of change, but not of progress.   The eighteenth century, however, did get the notion of historic change affecting the structure of social affairs for the better.   That is what we mean by progress. It was Darwin, a hundred years later, who most of all gave the modern conception of change.   To use James's phrase, he took the lid off the universe.   Change became possible in fundamental affairs.   Social dynamics, as opposed to social statics, became the object of our most significant study; and a new logic that puts change inherent in life, gives it a significant place, becomes necessary if we are going to deal with life as we have it.

4. *The free play of intelligence is our final resource to tell us what to think and do in all human affairs.*

Do not let the word "play" trouble you.   Children's play is not the oldest use of the word "play."   The play of light and shade on a stream as the light comes through the trees gives a truer meaning of the term.   The play of intelligence is the directing of intelligence to whatever one may be concerned with.   This principle asserts that the free play of intelligence, the unimpeded action of intelligence, is our final resource.   This defines at once our most inclusive social and educational aim.   Intelligence here means the ability to manage an actual situation.   As an honorific term it means the superior ability so to manage.   How intelligence in any effectual sense is in largest measure a social product was discussed in the preceding chapter.

To say that the free play of intelligence is our final resource does not mean that we are to follow the private unaided intelligence even of the genius, still less of

every hardboiled cocksure self-seeker. Rather does it
mean that it is intelligence, criticized intelligence, that
is to tell us what to think and do, not authority of the
state, church, or tradition. The free play of intelligence means, further, that it is criticized intelligence
which is to tell us whether we have or have not proved
anything, whether we do or do not know anything. In
other words, the free play of intelligence means that
unhindered and unimpeded study, as intelligently directed as we possibly can manage, is the best method we
know of finding out what to do and think. If any would
propose to state boundaries in advance and say that we
must not go beyond this line in what we shall study or
hear or consider, then he is by so much choosing to ignore intelligence. He is preaching unintelligence.

This fourth principle of the free play of intelligence
is bound up with the third principle, that of change.
When men believed that truth existed prior to man
and independently of man, and when they believed in
scientific laws that controlled phenomena, when man
believed these static ideas, it was easy, almost inevitable,
that the *status quo* should claim for itself that it had
found those unvarying truths and those unchangeable
laws; and it was easy, therefore, for the upholders of the
status quo to say that any questioning of it was immoral
and unpatriotic and that any new proposal was subversive. This word "subversive" deserves to be put in quotations whenever used, and you will find that it is
generally used by people who hold to the older doctrine
of change and who deny what I have just said about the
free play of intelligence. Under those conditions, any

questioning was easily believed, at least by the proponents of the *status quo,* to be unpatriotic; and all 'isms
except Americanism (as "we" hold it) were therefore
wrong and must be fought. The upholders of the *status
quo* claimed that whatever was, was the only right thing;
the existing order is the only order, and all else is chaos.

Now, all of these wrong notions easily followed from
having static ideas fixed in advance. This principle of
the free play of intelligence is thus back of our constitutional provision for free speech and a free press and
back of our demand for free study in schools and col-
leges; and democracy as a government is the effort to
make the free play of intelligence rule in governmental
affairs. In a developing world, new problems will arise.
New thinking becomes a necessity. Unhindered study
is the only way to make intelligence prevail, and no lines
can be drawn in advance as to what study will or will
not be rewarding. Actual search is the only way to tell
what is worth studying and no Mayor Hague nor his
backers has a right to tell us not to study.

Since these things are true for the citizens responsible
now for affairs, it becomes incumbent upon people to
learn how to study, how to study so as to make intelligence rule, to learn how to study live problems; for
only by the study of current live problems can people
learn how to study them. Thus, current controversial
issues, as I said earlier, become an essential for the
school and for democracy. When the president-general
of one of these "patriotic" societies said that "academic
freedom of speech has no place in school, where the
youth of our country are taught and their unformed

minds are developing," she had in mind that a school is properly a place that forms the minds of children to think what "we" agree that they ought to think. But the free play of intelligence means that a school is an institution that tries to get pupils to the place where they can themselves think, where they can increasingly think as they grow older, each for himself, and that tries to get the students to the place ultimately where each will be able and disposed to find out any weak points in what we, his elders, have hitherto thought. Unless we can get our pupils and students ultimately to the place where they can improve upon us, we have not done fairly by them. This president-general believed, apparently, in indoctrination and not in education. She believed in indoctrinating ideas into our young so that when they are old they will not depart therefrom. She wanted them to stay there against the probability of change in order that the *status quo* might be maintained, right or wrong, good or bad. But education in the full sense frees one to think, frees him not to follow whims, not to think as he pleases (so to speak), but frees him to wish the intelligent way and to seek it and, better still, to find it. It frees him from prejudice as far as we can effect it, frees him by giving him fruitful methods of study, frees him to wish that his wishes may themselves follow only intelligence.

As we think of these things, we see that we owe final allegiance not to what we have hitherto thought, and not to what the wisest and best among us have hitherto thought or think they have proved. We owe allegiance to the best that thinking can find out from now on, and not to what has been found out. Now, this is not a formula with which to run wild, to seek change for the mere sake of change. It is rather a formula to learn to study honestly, to study both what now is and what is proposed to be; and to wish the best that thinking can find out, whether this best be new or old.

5. *The fifth principle is that democracy is the effort to run society on the basis of the principles up to this time enumerated.* Democracy seeks enriched life for all people because life is good. It proposes to respect personality in all that it does and on terms of equality as far as it honestly can. Democracy knows that change is inherent in human affairs, and it proposes to follow intelligence in trying to direct that change in order to bring as far as possible the good life for all concerned. We need not further discuss democracy, because it simply sums up what the other principles have developed.

6. *Society can no longer run itself on the individualistic basis of each man for himself alone.*

Of course, to run a society along such lines was never good morals nor good religion, but it was good business; and there was a time in American history when *laissez faire* seemed productive of the best living for all. That was a time of self-sufficient farm life and of unlimited free lands. That day has passed. Scientific invention, factories producing on the basis of division of labor, and large corporations owning many factories—these things have brought it about that the farmer no longer produces mainly for home consumption, but mainly to sell. The wheat farmer sells his wheat and buys his flour or perhaps his bread, or even his bread cut into slices ready to be toasted; and he will buy this along with nearly everything else that he and his family use. The farmer, then, instead of being independent as formerly, is now dependent on the market and on business conditions.

And if the farmer has become dependent on business conditions, much more so are all those who work in factories or in the transportation of goods or in the selling of goods. If business conditions are bad, these people may lose their positions and cannot buy. The depression showed how we have all been brought to a common state of interdependence; all are now dependent on the industrial system. Under these new conditions, we must study our institutions and restudy the problem of rights. As stated earlier, all institutional arrangements (including all things we call rights) are to be judged by the way they work, by the way they do or do not bring the good life equally to all men. If, under these new conditions, there are new institutional arrangements and different conceptions of what should constitute right that promise to bring better life to all than now obtains, then it becomes our duty to study out all that is there involved and to decide democratically what to do and democratically to do it.

Among these institutional arrangements and ideas to be studied is democracy itself. It cannot escape study. It cannot escape possible revision and remaking. To ask that it be not studied, to say that it cannot be revised, is undemocratic. I admit I cannot conceive that intelligent study will change substantially the general prin-

ciples that I have already stated: namely, respect for
personality, substantial equality as an aim, the free play
of intelligence as our guide. I cannot myself see any
probability that further study will question these; but
I owe allegiance not to what I have hitherto thought but
rather to what better study can find out. So I must ask
for a restudy of democracy under the new conditions,
an honest restudy of its several principles; and I must
not be surprised if, amid other great changes, some of
the things that we have hitherto prized under the name
of democracy have to be given up. For one thing, possibly unlimited property rights; for another, possibly (I
do not know) our competitive business system. I do not
know, but I must encourage study if I am honest; and I
am reasonably sure that we must look forward to considerable planning, with much more co-operative and
collective responsibility for the common good than we
have thus far known. The time may very possibly come
when we can no longer wait around for "confidence" to
revive business conditions and start adequate production. Instead, we ourselves may decide to start production on a basis not dependent on "confidence." But, I
repeat, all of those things and other like decisions belong
as yet to the dimly seen, but probably not distant, future. The decisions, I hope, will be made only democratically, after free and full study. And, again, I know
that I do not know the answers to the study.

7. *The conscious improving of our culture should be
a chief determining goal of both social and educational
endeavor.*

The culture includes all the stored-up knowledge and

contrivances of human history. It thus constitutes that framework within which men live together. In this way it is the chief educative factor to determine how men shall think and act. Every baby is born into an already existent culture. From his family and the close community he learns their language, their manner of living, their customs, their ways of thinking, and in greatest measure, their standards and values for judging life and conduct.

Any adequate culture represents a balanced whole: Part fits with part to care for the whole round of life. Where any civilization remains long undisturbed, within and without, its culture will tend to approach such a balanced whole. So it was with Western Europe in the thirteenth century; so it was with China before 1800; so it was in considerable degree in this country during the early national period.

But when, as now with us, certain parts of the culture grow very rapidly (e.g., the scientific and the technological), then some other parts closely dependent on these also will grow rapidly, but other parts will lag. In this way come social strains and consequent social problems; and these, if they increase sufficiently, will endanger our civilization.

It is the combined effect of these two facts relating to the culture that fix for the educator this seventh aim as stated. On the one hand, the culture is very, very powerful to mold all to its model. On the other, when our culture is divided, certain parts work against other parts. Our civilization is distraught. The conscious improving of the culture consequently becomes an urgent guiding aim for education.

It appears clear from many considerations that the social-economic-political area sets today the main problem for our civilization. We can produce as never before. In fact, we can produce so much that we cannot sell it. Yet one-third of our people, we are told, are ill fed, ill housed, ill clothed. And at the bottom of the scale ten millions are out of employment. The social-political problem of distributing our goods lags far behind the problem of production. We could, it appears, produce enough not only to banish all poverty, but to provide reasonable comfort for all. But we do not, and we do not seriously try.

Many signs indicate that we are in the midst of a great social revolution, peaceful we hope, but still probably very far-reaching. How to steer this social change along desirable lines, that is the great problem. My guess is that we shall be working practically at this problem for three half-generations, beginning with 1930. If so, education should play a great part, especially in the effort to build a higher social intelligence level. How to manage to build social intelligence and not indoctrinate is not easy. How to educate so that real progress will come—that is the great task.

There are two other principles that belong here to fill out the series: one relating to the nature of the culture and our need to improve it and the other relating to the learning process and how it goes on; but since these have already been considered in previous chapters, we need not consider them now.

In final summation, we start our philosophic thinking right where we find ourselves when we start. We start with our existing knowledge, with our existing active system of value. We trust to the intelligent criticism of this, as it goes on in experience, to improve itself. It is criticized experience that must tell us finally what to think and do. Even those who think they have some other resource than the free play of intelligence, in the end, justify their thinking by appeal to experience itself. Thus, criticized experience, it appears, is the bottom basis to which we all must appeal.

INDEX

Acceptance
Essential in learning, 89-90, 104-105
Builds character, 120-122
Adolescents
Education in democratic living, 106-116
Adult Education
And democracy, 41-56, 57-65
Future of, 57-65
Why needed, 45-56, 60-62
Aims in education
Basic, 100-105
American Dream
Referred to, 6
Authoritarianism
Basis of indoctrination? 159
Rejection of, 170-171, 175-177
Behavior
Nature of, 77-79
Change
Adjusting to, 169-170
Social significance of, 188-189
Social control of, 190-192, 193-197
Inherent in human affairs? 203-206
Character building
Discussed, 72-73, 74-76, 114, 117-131, 132-135
Nurture and nature, 117-120
Not by separate habits, 124-125
Thinking essential to, 125-126
Through all living, 126-127, 129
Rôle of adult, 130
Spoiling, 128, 155-156
Choice
Essential in democratic education, 108-109, 113
Clifford, W. K.
Quoted, 66, 84

Coercion
And learning, 97-98, 127-128
Concomitant learnings
Discussed, 75-76, 100-102
Controversial issues
Discussed, 39-40, 208
Referred to, 111
Co-operation
Co-operative community activities, 38
To social ends, 112
Culture, the
How it operates, 42-45
Explanation of "race" differences, 43-44, 181
At present unbalanced, 45-46, 47ff., 189-190
Basis of building intelligence, 182-186
Social improvement of, 212-215
Democracy
Defined, 1-3, 18-21, 210
Education for, 3, 22-23, 52-54, 106-116
To be maintained, 11-12, 14
How maintained, 14ff.
Outlook, 14-17
Discussed, 18-28
Ethical basis of, 18-21
And social change, 29-31, 46-48, 191, 211-212
And adult education, 41-56
Intelligence, Individual Differences, and Democracy, 179-187
Social change in, 195-197
Must be studied, 211-212
Dictatorship
Its weakness, 2
Its method, 2
Teacher in, 29